BASIC

BASIC

An Introduction to
Computer Programming
Using the BASIC Language

Third Edition

William F. Sharpe
Nancy L. Jacob

THE FREE PRESS
A Division of Macmillan Publishing Co., Inc.
NEW YORK

Collier Macmillan Publishers
LONDON

Copyright © 1979 by The Free Press
  A Division of Macmillan Publishing Co., Inc.

The Free Press
A Division of Macmillan Publishing Co., Inc.
866 Third Avenue, New York, N. Y. 10022

Collier Macmillan Canada, Ltd.

Library of Congress Catalog Card Number: 78-72148

Printed in the United States of America

printing number

            5   6   7   8   9   10

Library of Congress Cataloging in Publication Data

Sharpe, William F
    BASIC : an introduction to computer programming
using the BASIC language.

    Includes index.
    1.   Basic (Computer program language)
I.   Jacob, Nancy L., joint author.   II.   Title.
QA76.73.B3S45   1979   001.6'424   78-72148
ISBN 0-02-928380-9
ISBN 0-02-928390-6 pbk.

Contents

Preface

In recent years the electronic digital computer has been transformed from a device understood by members of a small cult of worshipers to an indispensable part of the life of every student, scientist, and businessman. Universities have taken account of its importance with courses on computers, systems analysis, computer programming, and more esoteric aspects of the field now known as computer science.

The key to an understanding of computers, and an essential skill for using them, is the knowledge of at least one computer programming language. There are many candidates. Some were developed when computers were both far more expensive and far less sophisticated than they are now. Such languages reduce the effort expended by the computer, but they often require substantial expenditures of time and effort by the user. Other languages take account of current technology and costs but were designed for limited classes of problems. Still others were designed for professional programmers willing and able to learn and remember rather complex sets of rules and restrictions.

This book describes a language that combines a number of desirable features with relatively few undesirable ones. The language is BASIC, developed at Dartmouth College under the direction of Professor J. G. Kemeny. It was designed for use with one of the first computer systems that allowed a number of people concurrently to communicate directly with the machine, using typewriter-like consoles. Since then, such *time-shared* computers have become commonplace. Many are available commercially, with costs as low as a few dollars per hour of use. It is literally true that a computer of this type is as near as the nearest telephone, because communication by means of standard telephone lines is the normal procedure for must commercial systems and many time-shared computers used by universities and private firms.

Recent advances in technology have led to the production of a number of relatively low cost desk-top computers, many of which can be programmed using the BASIC language. It is likely that past trends will continue; the day of the inexpensive hand-held computer that can be programmed in BASIC may not be far off.

BASIC is the major language used with many time-shared computer systems and desk-top computers. But it is also found in more conventional environments, with the user preparing instructions and data on punched cards and submitting them for processing as part of a batch of such jobs at a central computer facility.

This book is designed to allow the user to think of a computer as if the latter "understands" the BASIC language. Thus no details of any of the supporting systems are included. This makes the book particularly suited for those unable to use a computer system, because it allows them to concentrate on the computational and logical properties of a high-level computer language with relatively little concern for clerical details.

Very little is said about computers per se; the interested student is referred to any of the almost countless introductory texts or manuals on the subject.

BASIC can be approached on two levels — first, as a simple, yet powerful language for standard numeric processing; then as a rich language for efficiently describing a wide range of advanced applications involving both the manipulation of numbers and the manipulation of textual material. This book is organized to reflect the dichotomy. Part I provides a full description of the essential features of the language. It should suffice for those persons who are interested in obtaining an appreciation of computers, the ability to use them in their academic work, and/or sufficient understanding to communicate with computer people in later life. Part II is designed for those persons with deeper interests and/or the need to use computers for more complex tasks. It introduces procedures particularly useful to the mathematician or scientist (for example, matrix commands) as well as those particularly useful to the business student or social scientist (for example, string manipulation).

The average college student should be able to learn the material in part I with five to ten hours of classroom exposure and an equal investment in time spent preparing actual programs. In many instances it may be both feasible and desirable to forego some or all of the classroom time, relying instead on this book and the availability of helpful advice when the student encounters problems or questions. In the final analysis, the computer itself may be the best teacher.

An important feature of this edition is its conformance with the proposed American National Standard for Minimal BASIC.* Unless otherwise noted, all the material in part I is consistent with the specifications in this important document. Most computer implementations of the language conform closely to the standard, minimizing the changes required to employ the procedures described in part I on any particular machine.

At present there is no set of standards for extended elements of BASIC. In part II we present representative examples of such extensions. Although modifications may be required for some computer systems, the overall concepts are quite general. To the extent possible, we have tried to anticipate future standards and insure that the material is consistent with present standards for Minimal BASIC.

We believe that BASIC represents an excellent first (or only) computer language. It includes many of the logical and conceptual components found in other programming languages, while requiring a minimum of attention to housekeeping details. Moreover, students who have learned BASIC have little difficulty with other languages. The marketplace has provided ample evidence of the usefulness of BASIC. We know no better test.

*May 1977, American National Standards Institute, 1430 Broadway, New York 10018.

PART I

Minimal BASIC

CHAPTER 1

Introduction

The Computer and You

Imagine that you have a diligent, hard-working, and accurate, but totally unimaginative, clerical assistant. Since the assistant is so unimaginative, it is necessary for you to provide very precise sets of instructions (what to do) as well as data (what to do it to). To avoid any problems, you and the assistant have agreed upon a rather limited language—vocabulary and grammar—for stating your instructions. The language has the virtue that it admits no ambiguity. If you follow the rules when stating your desires, the assistant will do precisely what you have in mind. If any mistakes are made, they will necessarily be yours.

Now substitute *computer* for *clerical assistant*. Call the set of instructions a *program*. Call the language BASIC. Otherwise everything is the same.

The object of this book is to teach the grammar and vocabulary of BASIC. Although no computer actually "understands" BASIC directly, many computers have been taught (preconditioned) to act as if they do. The manner in which this was done need not concern the reader; for all practical purposes, one can assume that such computers understand BASIC.

Communication

To make a computer do your work, you must provide it with a *program* (indicating what to do), *data* (things to be processed), and certain information required to identify you, to tell the computer how important you are, where to send the bill, and so forth. All of this must be sent to the computer somehow,

3

and the computer must return information as well. Many installations provide users with typewriter-like consoles that can communicate with the computer either directly or over standard telephone lines. Others require that information be input from punched cards; output is then returned later on printed sheets. In some cases a user can communicate directly with a computer (usually a desk-top model) devoted entirely to his or her task. Detailed information about such matters obviously must be obtained from those with knowledge of the particular computer to be utilized. This book deals with the more essential and more general aspects—the writing of programs and the arrangement of data.

A program consists of a series of statements (instructions or commands); each is written on a separate line. The lines are numbered from top to bottom, with smaller numbers preceding larger numbers. Systems that allow the user to enter lines directly keep the lines in correct numeric sequence, even if they are not entered in order. When using punched-card input, the user may have to arrange the cards correctly himself, with lower-numbered cards preceding higher-numbered cards.

Data are prepared in a similar fashion. Each line containing data is numbered, and the set of lines is arranged in sequence, either automatically (for console entry systems) or by the user (for punched-card systems).

Nothing will be said here about operating teletypewriters, keypunch machines, desk-top computers, and so on. Such information is easy to obtain; the best method is simply to spend five minutes at a machine with someone who knows how to operate it.

Diagnostic Messages

As we have suggested, you can assume that the computer recognizes instructions written in the BASIC language. But what if you present it with an illegal instruction (i.e., one that violates the rules for grammar and vocabulary presented here)? In most cases the computer will be aware that it does not understand the instruction and make a reasonably well informed guess about the source of its (more properly, your) confusion. And it will tell you about its difficulty and provide its diagnosis of the problem. Don't be embarrassed by such *diagnostic messages;* most programmers learn more from them than from manuals.

Unfortunately, the computer can detect only errors arising from illegal vocabulary and/or grammar; it cannot read your mind. If your program is constructed according to the rules, the computer will happily do precisely what you tell it to do. It is up to you to make certain that what you tell it to do is what you want it to do.

Output

When you give a program and data to a computer, one or two operations take place. First, the computer looks over your program. If serious errors are found, it tells you about them (with alarming candor, on occasion), and then it refuses to have anything more to do with you until you correct the errors. On the other hand, if it finds your program acceptable, it meekly begins to follow your instructions, looking at your data when told to do so and providing answers in accordance with your instructions.

CHAPTER 2

Getting Started

Here are an extremely simple program and set of data.

Program

```
10    REM -- PAYROLL PROGRAM
20    REM -- PROGRAMMER, WALTER P. BUNCZAK
30    READ P
35    READ H
45    LET G = P * H
60    LET W = .14 * G
70    LET N = G - W
80    PRINT P
90    PRINT H
100   PRINT G
110   PRINT W
120   PRINT N
140   GO TO 30
```

[handwritten: " DUMMY DATA" TECHNIQUE]

[handwritten: 31 IF P<0 GOTO 999 OTHERWISE PROGRAM RUNS OUT OF DATA]

[handwritten: 31 IF P = -1 THEN GOTO 999]

Data

```
900   DATA  2.25
901   DATA 40
902   DATA  3.00
903   DATA 41
904   DATA  2.97
905   DATA 35
906   DATA  3.10
907   DATA 49
999   END
```

[handwritten: 908 -1, 0]

7

Format

To make a program easy to read we often insert spaces within statements. To avoid ambiguity, some separation is required. For example, key words such as READ, PRINT, and LET should be separated from numbers, letters, etc. by at least one space.[1] Moreover, such words should be typed without any intermediate spaces. So should numbers. A good rule is to simply do what comes naturally.

You may have to get used to capital letters. There are no lower-case letters on some input devices, and even if you can type them in, the computer may treat them as upper-case and type them back to you in that form. The major exception concerns letters typed between quotation marks — in such instances if you can type in lower-case letters, the computer will probably leave them alone.

Line Numbers

Notice that each statement in the program has a line number and that the numbers are arranged in order. Line numbers are required and should be between 1 and 9999. Only integers — whole numbers — are allowed. It is a good idea to leave gaps when assigning numbers (e.g., writing 10, 20, 30, and so on) in case you subsequently wish to insert additional statements.

Remarks

Every statement must begin with a legal command (after the line number). The first two commands in the program at the beginning of this chapter are remarks. A remark is used to provide information for you and/or anyone else reading your program; it provides no information to the computer. In fact, the computer ignores remarks (saying, in effect, "He or she is only talking to himself or herself, not to me"). To indicate a remark, simply use the command REM; after that you may write anything you please.

---

1. Key words in Minimal BASIC (all of which are described in this book) are: BASE, DATA, DEF, DIM, END, FOR, GO, GOSUB, GOTO, IF, INPUT, LET, NEXT, ON, OPTION, PRINT, RANDOMIZE, READ, REM, RESTORE, RETURN, STEP, STOP, SUB, THEN, and TO.

Instruction Sequence

A program is nothing more than a set of instructions (although remarks are instructions only in a rather academic sense). The computer is expected to follow the instructions in a particular order. If you are entering your program from a teletype or other remote terminal, the computer will execute your instructions sequentially by line number unless told to do otherwise. In other words, it will first execute the statement having the lowest line number, then the statement having the next higher line number, and so on, unless the statements themselves tell the computer to deviate from that order. (The instruction in line 140 of our sample program does just that, as you will see.) Only *one* statement can be executed at a time. All this means you must be careful to assign line numbers that accurately reflect the order in which you wish the statements in your program executed. And the order of execution is the main reason why it is important to obtain a listing of your program with the statements appearing in order by line number (as has been done with all the programs in this book). It makes the program much easier for humans to follow, since execution will proceed from the top of the page to the bottom.

Variables

The computer is provided with a number of "mailboxes," each of which can hold a number. Each mailbox has a name. There are twenty-six mailboxes with simple one-letter names: A, B, C, . . . , Z. Some other mailboxes have two-character names—a letter followed by a digit: A0, A1, . . . , A9, B0, . . . , B9, C0, . . . , Z9.

For convenience we often use the name of a mailbox to indicate the number in it. And because the number in a mailbox may be taken out and a new one put in its place, we often refer to the number in a mailbox as a variable (because it may vary as the program is executed). Thus variable A means the number currently in mailbox A; variable B3 means the number currently in mailbox B3.

Reading Data

The data on which a program operates often consist of a set of numbers. It is useful to think of the numbers as if they were in a list, with one item per row. At any given time there is a pointer indicating the next item to be read. Initially, it is set to point at the first item on the list. As the program proceeds, whenever one piece of data is used (read), the pointer moves down one item.

The DATA statements in our program may be thought of as providing the list of numbers for the computer. In this case the number 2.25 is at the top, the number 40 is next, and so on. The order is, as before, determined by the line number of the DATA statement; the DATA statement with the lowest line number will be the first to be used.

We are now in a position to understand statement 30 in the program. It says, "Take the number from the top of the data stack and put it in mailbox P, throwing away any number that might be there already." Thus after statement 30 has been executed the first time, the number 2.25 will be in mailbox P. It will have been "used," moving the pointer to the number 40, which is the next one in line.

What happens when the computer encounters statement 35? The next number in the list (40) is placed in mailbox H, and 3.00 is now the next in line.

We often describe this process in more elegant terms. For example, we might say that the *value* 2.25 has been *assigned to* variable P. Or, more explicitly, we might say that 2.25 has been *read into* P. In any event, the process is clear enough.

It should come as no surprise that P is being used to represent the hourly pay rate of some employee and H the number of hours he or she worked during the week. The object of the program is to compute the gross pay (G), withholding (W), and net pay (N). The computations are performed as specified by instructions 45, 60, and 70.

Expressions

Look at statement 45. The portion to the right of the equal sign is an *expression*. It specifies that certain *computations* are to be performed and a *value* obtained. To be specific, P * H says, "Multiply the number currently in mailbox P by the number currently in mailbox H; the result is the *value of the expression*." Notice that the numbers in P and H are *not* altered when the expression is evaluated.

Expressions are formed according to the standard rules of arithmetic. Five basic operations are available:

+	Addition
−	Subtraction
*	Multiplication
/	Division
∧	Exponentiation[2]

---

2. Some systems use an upward-pointing arrow (↑) or two asterisks (**) for this purpose.

Certain problems present themselves, however. Since the entire expression must be written on one line, ambiguities may arise. To divide A by the sum of B and C, you might say:

$$A/B + C$$

But this might be interpreted by the computer as the sum of A/B and C. It is possible to find out the rules the computer uses when there is an ambiguity, but why bother? Instead, just use parentheses to avoid any problems:

$$A/(B + C)$$

Expressions may be very complicated:

$$(C \wedge (A3/(B * X))) - Z5$$

or very simple:

$$X4$$

They may use variables and/or *constants*. A constant is simply a number written in the program. The rules for writing numbers apply to both constants and numbers included as data:

1. A decimal point may or may not be included.
2. A minus number is indicated by preceding the number with a minus sign.
3. A positive number need not be preceded by a plus sign.
4. Commas may *not* be included.

Some legal numbers are:

$$.01$$
$$.3$$
$$256.4$$
$$35$$
$$-1.257639$$

To summarize, an expression may be:

1. a variable or
2. a constant or
3. any combination of variables and/or constants connected by operators, with parentheses included when necessary to avoid ambiguity.

When an expression is evaluated, the current values of the variables (if any) are used, along with the constants (if any) to obtain a single value (number).[3] The values of the variables are *not* altered when the expression is evaluated.

LET Commands

The form of a LET command is:

LET *variable = expression*

It says, simply:

1. Evaluate the expression on the right-hand side of the equal sign.
2. Then insert that value in the mailbox (variable) indicated on the left-hand side of the equal sign, throwing away any value currently in the mailbox.

When the program reaches statement 45 for the first time, the current value of P (2.25) will be multiplied by H (40). The result (50) will then be placed in box G. The values of P and H are, of course, unchanged. After statement 45 has been executed, G will contain the gross pay for the individual being processed.

Statement 60 uses the value of G for further computation. It instructs the computer to multiply the current value of G (50) by .14; the result is then placed in box W. This is obviously the amount to be withheld.

Statement 70 calculates the individual's net pay (G − W) and inserts it in box N. The calculations are now complete

PRINT Commands

It does little good to perform calculations if the results are simply left in the computer where no one can see them. Thus we instruct the computer:

80   PRINT P

This means, simply, "Print the number in box P." Printing has no effect on the contents of the boxes; it merely allows the user to see what the contents are. The full set of instructions:

```
 80    PRINT  P
 90    PRINT  H
100    PRINT  G
110    PRINT  W
120    PRINT  N
```

3. In later chapters, to be more precise, we will call this an *arithmetic expression*, since it yields a numeric value.

causes the following numbers to be printed:

```
   2.25
 40
 90
 12.6
 77.4
```

Needless to say, this is hardly very elegant output. We will learn to improve it later; for the present, be content with the ability to get numbers out of the computer and onto the output sheet where you can see them.

GO TO Commands

Although it is comforting to know that the computer has accurately processed the payroll for the first employee (the one making $2.25 per hour), it would hardly be worthwhile to write a program to do so little work. Had we wanted no more from the computer, we could have said:

140   STOP

But there are other employees to be processed; we want to tell the computer to do to them what it did to the first employee. To do this we simply instruct it to alter the normal sequence in which it follows instructions:

140   GO TO 30

This says, simply, "Go back to statement 30, then proceed again in order until I tell you to do otherwise."[4]

What happens? The computer encounters statement 30, which instructs it to read the number at the top of the data stack (3.00) into location (variable, or mailbox) P; the former value (2.25) is thrown away in the process. The next statement instructs the computer to read the next data number (41) into H, and its former value is thrown away in the process. Then the computations are performed using the *current* values of P and H. Obviously, the resulting values of G, W, and N will be those applicable to the new employee. For example, when statement 45 is executed, P * H (3.00 * 41) will be placed in G and the former value thrown away. Thus G will equal 123—the second employee's gross pay for the week. W and N will be computed similarly. And the final results (including P and H, shown for the records) will be printed on the output sheet.

---

4. If desired, the space between GO and TO can be omitted, and the single key word GOTO used instead.

After the second employee's payroll has been printed, the computer will again reach statement 140 and will once again go back to statement 30. The third employee's pay will be processed, then the fourth, then the fifth, and so on. When will it all stop? When the computer runs out of numbers. Obviously no more can be done for you, so the computer will terminate your job.

The END Command

The last line in your program should have the key word END. This helps the computer by indicating the physical end of the material you are giving it. Moreover, if the computer reaches this line when running the program, it will stop.

Reprise

For all its simplicity, the program shown here could be used to compute gross pay, withholding, and net pay accurately and rapidly for a great many (thousands, if you wish) employees. Every week you could prepare a new set of data and get a completely different set of results using the same program. Needless to say, there is more to the BASIC language; you will soon be able to do many more things (and to do them more elegantly). But it is useful to learn to crawl before attempting to run. Try to answer the problems at the end of this chapter. If you can't, reread the material before looking at the answers provided. Then write some programs of your own using the portions of the language you now know. The computer can help you.

Problems

1. Find any errors in the following expressions:

    (a) 3
    (b) X
    (c) A0 + B3
    (d) AB/C
    (e) A + (B/C) * D
    (f) − 3 + X
    (g) (8 + Z2)/ − 6
    (h) A35 + C
    (i) 3X/D
    (j) (Q + I)W9
    (k) ((A + B)/(C − X) ∧ 8

(l) $3 * (A/ + 8)$

(m) $A \wedge .5$

2. What output would be produced if the set of data given for the payroll program (at the beginning of this chapter) were submitted with the following program?

```
  5     READ X
 10     READ Y
 15     READ Z
 20     READ Z2
100     PRINT X
105     PRINT Y
110     LET Q3 = X * Y
115     PRINT Q3
120     LET Z3 = Z2 - Z
125     PRINT Z3
150     GO TO 5
```

3. The value of a dollar at the end of N years compounded annually at an interest rate of 10 percent per year is:

$$value = 1.10 \wedge N$$

Write a program to read a set of values of N, producing for each one the value of a dollar at the end of that many years. Be certain to print N each time.

4. In a single LET statement, assign the value of the following expression to variable X:

$$X = \cfrac{Y + W}{\cfrac{Z}{(W * Y)} - \cfrac{(Y + 3)^2}{27.3}}$$

Be sure to use parentheses.

5. Write a complete program to do some sort of calculation, and prepare at least a few lines of data to test the program. When preparing your program:

   (a) Follow the sample program in this chapter fairly closely.

   (b) Limit your computations to relatively simple combinations of basic operations, using parentheses whenever there might be any ambiguity concerning your intentions.

   (c) Be certain that your program will terminate, either by reaching a STOP statement or by running out of data.

   (d) Try not to be too ambitious the first time. You may want to build confidence by merely copying the sample program and adding one or two extra computations and outputs.

(e) If your program will not run, read the diagnostic messages from the computer, make the necessary corrections, and try again.

(f) If the program runs but produces incorrect answers, play computer: Follow your own instructions until you find the error in your logic. Then correct the program and try again.

Answers

1. (a) This is perfectly legal; a constant is a valid expression.

   (b) This is legal, too; a variable is a valid expression.

   (c) This is legal; A0 is a valid variable name, as is B3. The value of this expression will be the sum of the numbers currently in boxes A0 and B3.

   (d) Illegal. A is a variable name, as is B. If the programmer had meant to multiply A times B, he or she should have said so:

$$(A * B)/C$$

   If you thought that AB was a valid variable name, you need to reread the chapter.

   (e) This is perfectly legal; however, it is ambiguous. If the programmer intended to multiply D by the sum of A and (B/C) then he or she should have added some more parentheses, *e.g.*:

$$(A + (B/C)) * D$$

   If you want to know what the computer will in fact do when there is ambiguity, the rules in most systems are:

   (1) Expressions inside parentheses are evaluated first.

   (2) Within a set of parentheses (or, if there are none, within the entire expression):

       a)   all exponentiation ($\wedge$) is performed first, from left to right.

       b)   multiplications (*) and divisions (/) are performed next, from left to right.

       c)   additions (+) and subtractions ($-$) are performed last, from left to right.

   Follow this set of rules to see how the computer would have handled the expression in this case of the programmer had *not* added more parentheses.

   (f) This is legal; -3 is treated as a constant.

(g) This may or may not be legal, depending on the system used. The constant -6 conforms to the rules; however, the fact that the division operator $(/)$ is next to the minus sign may cause a diagnostic message, because a minus sign is also used to indicate subtraction. To avoid such a possibility, it is a good idea to throw in extra parentheses:

$$(8 + Z2)/(-6)$$

The general rule is to avoid situations in which two operators are next to each other.

(h) This is illegal. A35 is not a valid variable name. The computer will probably think that you have put a variable (A3) next to a constant (5). Whatever the computer thinks it has found, it won't like it.

(i) This is illegal, too. If the programmer meant 3 times X, he or she should have said so:

$$(3 * X)/D$$

(j) Same problem. Multiplication must be indicated explicitly:

$$(Q + I) * W9$$

(k) The parentheses fail to pair up here. To avoid this kind of error it is useful to check complicated expressions, using the following scheme. Read the expression from left to right, keeping a cumulative count. Start the count at 0. Whenever you find a left parenthesis, — add one to the count. Whenever you find a right parenthesis, — subtract one. The count should never become negative and should be zero when you reach the end of the expresison. If not, you have made a mistake. If you don't find it, the computer will.

(l) As in (g), this expression may or may not be legal, depending on the system used, because the computer may be confused by the two adjacent operators. To cure this drop the plus sign, because it is redundant:

$$3 * (A/8)$$

(m) Perfectly legal in Minimal BASIC: the value of this expression will be the square root of A. However, some systems may balk at such an expression since they can only handle whole numbers as exponents. If so, functions, described in chapter 8, can be used to accomplish the purpose.

2.
$$2.25$$
$$40$$
$$90$$
$$38$$
$$2.97$$
$$35$$
$$103.95$$
$$45.90$$

3. There are, of course, many ways to write a program designed to accomplish any given task. The important point is to write one that works (whether or not it is "efficient" is clearly a secondary matter). A program to compute the values specified for this problem follows:

```
10    READ N
20    PRINT N
30    LET V = 1.10^N
40    PRINT V
50    GO TO 10
60    END
```

4. Don't be afraid to use parentheses liberally. One way to write the statement is:

$$\text{LET } X = (Y + W)/((Z/(W * Y)) - ((Y + 3)\quad 2)/27.3)$$

5. Good luck.

CHAPTER 3

Conditional Transfers

The program in chapter 2 was fine for determining pay and withholding for each individual on the payroll. Reduced to its fundamentals, the program looked like that shown in figure 3.1.

This is a classic example of a *loop*—the main reason that it pays people to write computer programs. In essence, we told the computer what to do for the first person on the payroll and then instructed it to loop back, read new data, repeat the computation, print the results, loop back, and so forth. The computer gets out of this loop by following the sensible rule that whenever it runs out of data there is nothing to do but give up.

The IF-THEN Command

You may not want the machine merely to stop after reading all the payroll data. Perhaps you would like to have it finish with a summary of the number of persons paid, total amount paid, and total amount withheld. To do this you need a *conditional transfer*—a statement that tells the computer to go (transfer) somewhere if (but only if) a certain condition is met.

Remember the way in which we set up the payroll data—each person's hourly pay rate was followed by the number of hours he or she worked during the week. After processing each person, the computer returned to process the next one. Our problem is to find some way to tell it when all the people have been processed. One way to do this is simply to add an unusual person at the end—one with an hourly rate of, say, −1 per hour, who worked, say −40 hours. Knowing that such a person will be the last in the set of data, we can

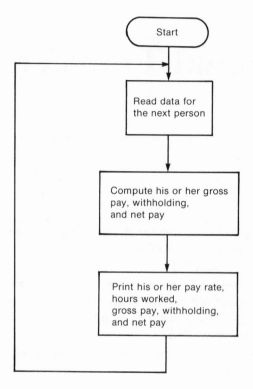

Figure 3.1

instruct the computer to watch out for him or her and then to transfer to a set of instructions for preparing summary information.

The new arrangement is shown in figure 3.2.

After reading each pair of numbers, we tell the computer to look at the number it put in box P. If it is not negative, the numbers referred to a real person and are to be processed accordingly. But if the number read into box P was negative, the numbers did not refer to a real person; they were a signal to indicate that the last person had already been processed. When this condition takes place, we want the computer to transfer out of the loop and print the desired summary information.

The new program follows:

```
10    REM --- A MORE IMPRESSIVE PAYROLL PROGRAM
11    REM --- PROGRAMMER: DAVID MATTHEWS
12    REM ------------------------------------
20    REM -- GET READY FOR PROCESSING
21    LET N1 = 0
22    LET T1 = 0
23    LET T2 = 0
25    REM ------------------------------------
30    REM -- READ DATA FOR THE NEXT PERSON
31    READ P
32    READ H
35    REM ------------------------------------
40    REM -- TEST FOR COMPLETION
41    IF P < 0 THEN 100
45    REM ------------------------------------
50    REM -- COMPUTE THIS PERSON'S PAYROLL
51    LET G = P*H
52    LET W = .14*G
53    LET N = G - W
55    REM ------------------------------------
60    REM -- PRINT HIS OR HER PAYROLL
61    PRINT P
62    PRINT H
63    PRINT G
64    PRINT W
65    PRINT N
68    REM ------------------------------------
70    REM -- COUNT AND ADD PAY AND WITHHOLDING TO TOTALS
71    LET N1 = N1+1
72    LET T1 = T1+N
73    LET T2 = T2+W
75    REM ------------------------------------
80    REM -- GO BACK TO READ MORE DATA
81    GOTO 30
90    REM ------------------------------------
100   REM -- THIS POINT REACHED WHEN ALL PERSONS PROCESSED
102   PRINT N1
103   PRINT T1
104   PRINT T2
110   STOP
120   END
```

The conditional transfer in the program is:

41   IF P < 0 THEN 100

Its meaning is: "If the current value of (the number in the box named) P is less than (<) zero, then go to line number 100. If it is not, proceed to the line that follows this statement (i.e., number 45)."

In general, a condition compares the values of two expressions. Of course, either expression may be simply a variable or a constant. Six types of comparison are possible:

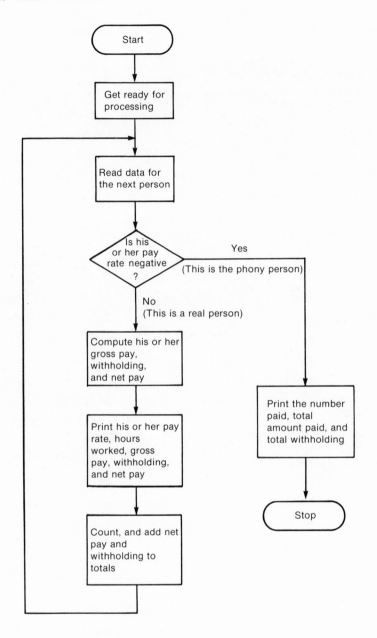

Figure 3.2

Comparison	Read as
>	"is greater than"
<	"is less than"
=	"is equal to"
> =	"is greater than or equal to"
< =	"is less than or equal to"
< >	{"is less than or greater than" / "is not equal to"}

The following examples illustrate the way in which the conditional transfer is used:

Statement	Meaning
IF A = G THEN 193	If the current value of A is equal to the current value of G, go to line number 193. If not, proceed.
IF A < > G THEN 503	If the current value of A does not equal the current value of G, go to line number 503. If it does, proceed.
If N > 100 THEN 324	If the current value of N is greater than 100, go to line number 324. If it is not (i.e., it is less than or equal to 100), proceed.
IF N > = 100 THEN 433	If the current value of N is greater than or equal to 100, go to line number 433. If it is not (i.e., it is less than 100), proceed.
IF W < 5 THEN 234	If the current value of W is less than 5, go to line number 234. If it is not (i.e., it is greater than or equal to 5), proceed.
IF W < = 5 THEN 235	If the current value of W is less than or equal to 5, go to line number 235. If it is not (i.e., it is greater than 5), proceed.

The quantities to be compared may be very complicated expressions. But (as always) be certain to use parentheses whenever there might be any ambiguity. For example:

$$IF \ A > (B - C) \ THEN \ 500$$
$$IF \ (8 - C) * B < 34 \ THEN \ 200$$
$$IF \ (3 * A) - (B \wedge 2) = Q \wedge 8 \ THEN \ 300$$

You should also be sure there really is another statement in your program with the line number referred to by an IF statement; the computer may be displeased if it is told to go to a nonexistent statement.

As you may have noticed, all the IF statements appearing so far in this chapter have conformed to the following general structure:

IF *expression comparison expression* THEN *line number*

This structure is legal in all systems; therefore, you can be certain that IF statements written in strict accordance with it will be accepted by the computer. Modifications allowed by some systems will be discussed in chapter 12; for now it is best to avoid any IF statement not fitting the structure.

The New Program

Initialization

Before the first person's payroll is processed, the number of personnel paid (to be recorded in box N1), the total amount paid out (to be recorded in box T1), and the total amount withheld (to be recorded in box T2) should all be zero. Statements 21, 22, and 23 set these variables to their initial values (zero). Statement 21, for example, says "Put the number 0 in box N1." Most loops are preceded by one or more such initialization instructions. Whenever a statement in a program refers to the current value of a variable (e.g., by using it in an expression), the variable should either have been previously initialized to some value by a LET statement or have been assigned a value from data by a READ statement. The computer may balk at trying to evaluate an expression when you have not told it what value to assign to one of the variables. Some computers will merely take the value that has not been initialized to be zero; others will use an arbitrary value left over from a previous program; yet others will complain to you and then quit. In any event, it is good practice to initialize all your variables yourself.

Reading the Data

The READ statements are similar to those in the earlier program. The first time through the loop, the first two numbers from the data list are read. The second time through, the next two are read; and so on.

Conditional Transfer

This is our new statement. If the numbers just read included a negative pay rate, the computer is supposed to go to line number 100. If not, it proceeds (to line number 45).

Computing and Printing Pay and Withholding

If the computer has read real payroll data into P and H, it will not transfer to statement 100 when it looks at P. Instead, it will proceed to compute the person's pay and withholding and print the results. The required statements (50 through 53 and 60 through 65) are, of course, similar to those used in the first payroll program.

Adding to Totals

After computing the pay and withholding for a new employee, we want to record the fact that we have paid one more person. To do this we write:

71   LET N1 = N1 + 1

In essence, this says: "Take the number currently in box N1, add one to it, then put the result in box N1 (throwing out the previous value)." Obviously N1 is serving as a *counter*—every time a new person's pay is processed, N1 is increased (or stepped up) by one. When the last pair of numbers is reached and the computer transfers to statement 100, N1 will equal the total number of people paid.

The other instructions keep the cumulative sums of pay and withholding. The statement:

72   LET T1 = T1 + N

says: "Take the number currently in box T1, add it to this person's net pay (N), and put the results in Box T1 (throwing out the previous value)." When the last pair of numbers is reached and the computer transfers to statement 100, T1 will equal the total amount paid out.

The third statement (73) takes care of withholding; when statement 100 is reached, T2 will equal the sum of the amounts withheld.

Printing Summary Information

The section of the program starting with statement 100 is reached only after a negative pay rate is read. The next three statements (102, 103, and 104) print the desired summary information. Since no more work remains to be done, we tell the computer to STOP.

Style

Some additional points are worth mentioning before leaving this example. First, notice the many remarks used to remind the reader of the programmer's intentions. If anything, there are too few remarks here. Good practice would dictate that the programmer identify the meaning attached to various key variables. For example:

15   REMARK – – P = PAY RATE IN DOLLARS PER HOUR

Notice also the number of remarks with dashes used to set off different sections of the program.

These are good habits. They require relatively little time when you are writing a program, and they may save a great deal of time later on.

Multiple Conditions

We have seen that the conditional transfer can be used to branch to a desired point in the program if some condition is met. But you may want to branch if any one of *several* conditions is met. It is not possible in Minimal BASIC to specify more than one condition per IF statement, so several IF statements may have to be used. Assume that a special procedure is required for employees with more than two dependents or with a gross pay exceeding $200 per week. If this special procedure begins at line number 300, the program could include the following statements:

```
100   IF D > 2 THEN 300
101   IF G > 200 THEN 300
```

Obviously, a number of other conditions could be added. If any were met, the computer would transfer to line number 300. If none was met, it would proceed to the next statement (i.e., the one following the last IF statement).

Take another case. Assume that a procedure is to be followed if (and only if) a number of conditions are all met. For example, the amount to be withheld might be zero if an employee had more than three dependents *and* earned *under* $100 per week. If both conditions are not met, some alternative procedure beginning with line number 250 is to be followed. This situation can be represented in a manner similar to that shown in the previous example:

```
201   IF D <= 3 THEN 250
202   IF G >= 100 THEN 250
203   LET W = 0
```

By carefully arranging conditional transfers, you can represent virtually any type of multiple condition. As always, it pays to check the logic by playing computer, following your instructions with test data to insure that they do what you want them to do.

The ON Command

Sometimes you will want a program to transfer to one of several locations, depending on the circumstances. For example, assume that associated with each member of a pension plan is a code indicating whether he or she is full time (code 1), part-time (code 2), or retired (code 3). Let's say that instructions for dealing with full-time employees begin at line 500, those for part-time employees begin at line 600, and those for retired employees begin at line 700. If the code for an employee has been read into box C, the desired effect can be obtained with the command:

ON C   GO TO 500, 600, 700

The general form of the ON command is:[1]

ON *expression*   GO TO *line number, line number, . . . , line number*

When a command of this type is reached, the *expression* is evaluated and rounded to the nearest whole number. If the value is 1, the program transfers to the first line number given; if the value is 2, the program transfers to the second line number; and so on. You may include as many line numbers as you wish. Just be certain that the value of the expression will never be less than 1 or more than the number of line numbers that you have included.

Problems

1. What is wrong with this set of instructions?

```
100    IF G < 200 THEN 120
110    LET T = .14 * G
120    LET T = 0
130    LET N = G - T
```

2. The computer is in the midst of a program. At the moment, the current values of key variables are:

---

1. Some nonstandard systems use slightly different forms, for example:

GO TO *expression* OF *line number, line number, . . ., line number*

A   3.5
B3   − 5.6
Z   100.2
Q2   0
F   1
K   − 4.2
T9   100.2

For each of the following statements, decide whether or not the computer will transfer to statement 500:
(a) IF A > F THEN 500
(b) IF A < F THEN 500
(c) IF B3 < K THEN 500
(d) IF Z < T9 THEN 500
(e) IF Z < = T9 THEN 500
(f) IF Q2 > B3 − K THEN 500

3. What, if anything, is wrong with each of the following statements?
   (a) ON 3   GO TO 100, 150, 200
   (b) ON X   GO TO 100, Y, Z

4. Under what conditions (i.e., for what values of A and B) will the following program segment assign the value one to variable T?

```
10    IF  A  <= 50  THEN  90
15    IF  A  > 100  THEN  90
20    IF  B  <= 50  THEN  90
25    IF  B  > 100  THEN  90
30    LET T = 1
35    GO TO 100
90    LET T = 0
100   PRINT T
```

5. The rules actually followed when computing the amount to be withheld for federal income tax are rather involved. The amount to be withheld depends on: (a) whether the taxpayer is single or married; (b) the number of allowances claimed; and (c) the amount earned. Assume that the data to be processed include the following information for each employee (in the order specified): (a) hourly pay rate; (b) the number of hours worked during the last *two* weeks; (c) the digit 0 (if single) or the digit 1 (if married); and (d) the number of allowances claimed. The following tables indicate the rules that might be used by a typical firm.

Single Persons

If the amount of wages during a two-week period (after allowing $28.80 for each allowance) is		The amount of income tax to be withheld shall be	
Not over $65		0	
Over	But not over		of excess over
$ 65	$152	16%	$ 65.00
152	267	18	74.67
267	363	22	113.27
363	440	24	134.08
440	594	28	177.79
594	710	32	229.81
710	—	36	283.17

Married Persons

If the amount of wages during a two-week period (after allowing $28.80 for each allowance) is		The amount of income tax to be withheld shall be	
Not over $121		0	
Over	But not over		of excess over
$ 121	$ 210	15%	$121.00
210	445	18	135.83
445	556	22	192.05
556	710	25	235.72
710	863	28	286.54
863	1017	32	358.59
1017	—	36	431.75

Write a program to read the information on each employee and compute the amount to be withheld from his or her income for the two-week period.

6. Make up some data to go with the program you wrote when answering problem 4. Be sure to include at least one person falling in each of the categories indicated in the rules for withholding. Then run your program and check its results with hand computations. This will prove to be time-consuming, but it constitutes an acid test of your program. It will also give you

a real appreciation for the power of the computer (and the advantages de-rived from being able to program it).

7. Now program something that interests you. Be certain that your program will terminate either by reaching a STOP statement or by running out of data. Run the program with real or test data. And keep at it until the pro-gram really works.

Answers

1. Presumably, the programmer wants to let T equal 0 if G is less than 200, and to let T equal .14 * G otherwise. The first goal is clearly met, but the second is not. To see why, assume that G is greater than 200. The condi-tion in statement 100 is not met, so the computer proceeds to statement 110, which sets T equal to .14 * G. So far, so good. But then the computer goes on to statement 120 which tosses out the current (desired) value of T and puts zero in instead. Obviously, the computer should be told to skip statement 120 in this case. A solution to the problem follows:

```
100    IF G < 200 THEN 120
110    LET T = .14 * G
115    GO TO 130
120    LET T = 0
130    LET N = G - T
```

2. (a) 3.5 is greater than 1; the computer will transfer to statement 500.
   (b) 3.5 is not less than 1; the computer will not transfer to statement 500.
   (c) -5.6 is less than -4.2; the computer will transfer to statement 500. Think of numbers as lying along a scale:

$$-5.6 \qquad -4.2 \qquad 0 \qquad +5$$

If one number lies to the right of another, we say it is greater; if it lies to the left, we say it is smaller.
   (d) 100.2 is not less than 100.2; thus the computer will not transfer to statement 500.
   (e) 100.2 is not less than 100.2, but it is equal to it; as long as either is true, the computer will transfer to statement 500.
   (f) Zero is greater than $-5.6-(-4.2) = -1.4$; the computer will transfer to statement 500.

3. (a) This is a perfectly legal ON statement, but it is rather silly. The same result could have been obtained by simply writing:

GO TO 200

(b) This is thoroughly illegal. You can only GO TO a line number, and Y and Z are variables, not line numbers.

4. The conditions are that both A and B must be greater than 50 but less than or equal to 100. The program establishes that these conditions are met by a process of elimination; if either A or B has a value outside the acceptable range there is no further checking.

5. There are many possible ways to program this. The version shown below is just one of them. After data for an employee are read (statements 10 through 13), his or her gross pay (G) and taxable income (T) are computer. These computations are required for all employees and are thus performed first. If the employee is married, processing begins with statement 100; if not, processing begins with statement 30.

In either case the first step is to see if any withholding is required. If not, withholding (W) is set to zero and the computer is instructed to go directly to the section for final processing (beginning with statement 200). If so, the income bracket is found by *successively checking to see if T is less than increasingly larger* amounts. To see why this works, consider a single employee with a gross income of $300. The computer will not transfer to statement 50 when it follows the instruction at statement 41. The mere fact that statement 42 is reached thus guarantees that income exceeds $152. But if the income is not less than or equal to $267, the computer will proceed to statement 43. The fact that statement 43 is reached indicates that the employee is single and has an income greater than $267. If income is also less than $363 (as we assume it is in this case), the computer will transfer to statement 70, which indicates the relevant amount to be withheld. Then the computer is told to transfer to the final portion of the program (located at statement 200).

The general procedure for finding the appropriate amount to be withheld is to pass through a number of IF statements involving less and less stringent requirements. When the appropriate bracket is found, the condition will be met and the computer will transfer to the relevant instruction. If none of the tests is met (e.g., if the employee is single and earns over $710), the statement following the last IF statement will be reached.

The final section of this program simply computes the employee's net pay, prints the results, and then transfers back to process a new employee. These operations are the same for all employees and are thus written only once.

```
1       REM -- WITHHOLDING PROGRAM
2       REM -------------------------------
5       REM -- READ DATA
10      READ P
11      READ H
12      READ M
13      READ A
15      REM -------------------------------
20      REM -- COMPUTE GROSS PAY AND TAXABLE INCOME
21      LET G = P * H
22      LET T = G - (28.8*A)
23      REM -------------------------------
25      REM -- SEE WHETHER MARIED OR SINGLE
26      IF M = 1 THEN 100
30      REM -------------------------------
31      REM -- EMPLOYEE IS SINGLE
32      REM -------------------------------
33      REM -- CHECK TO SEE IF TAX MUST BE WITHHELD
34      IF T > 65 THEN 40
35      REM -- NO WITHHOLDING REQUIRED
36      LET W = 0
37      GOTO 200
40      REM -- WITHHOLDING REQUIRED, FIND BRACKET
41      IF T <= 152 THEN 50
42      IF T <= 267 THEN 60
43      IF T <= 363 THEN 70
44      IF T <= 440 THEN 80
45      IF T <= 594 THEN 90
46      IF T <= 710 THEN 95
47      LET W = .36*(T-283.17)
48      GOTO 200
50      LET W = .16*(T-65)
51      GOTO 200
60      LET W = .18*(T-74.67)
61      GOTO 200
70      LET W = .22*(T-113.67)
71      GOTO 200
80      LET W = .24*(T-134.08)
81      GOTO 200
90      LET W = .28*(T-177.79)
91      GOTO 200
95      LET W = .32*(T-229.81)
96      GOTO 200
100     REM -------------------------------
101     REM -- EMPLOYEE IS MARRIED
102     REM -------------------------------
103     REM -- CHECK TO SEE IF TAX MUST BE WITHHELD
104     IF T > 121 THEN 110
105     REM -- NO WITHHOLDING REQUIRED
106     LET W = 0
107     GOTO 200
110     REM -- WITHHOLDING REQUIRED, FIND BRACKET
111     IF T <= 210 THEN 130
112     IF T <= 445 THEN 140
113     IF T <= 556 THEN 150
114     IF T <= 710 THEN 160
115     IF T <= 863 THEN 170
116     IF T <= 1017 THEN 180
120     LET W = .36*(T-431.75)
121     GOTO 200
130     LET W = .15*(T-121)
131     GOTO 200
140     LET W = .18*(T-135.83)
141     GOTO 200
150     LET W = .22*(T-192.05)
151     GOTO 200
160     LET W = .25*(T-235.72)
161     GOTO 200
```

```
170    LET W = .28*(T-286.54)
171    GOTO 200
180    LET W = .32*(T-358.59)
181    GOTO 200
200    REM ------------------------------
201    REM - COMPUTE NET PAY AND PRINT RESULTS
210    LET N = G - W
211    PRINT P
212    PRINT H
213    PRINT G
214    PRINT W
215    PRINT N
220    REM ------------------------------
221    REM -- RETURN TO PROCESS NEXT PERSON
222    GOTO 5
9999   END
```

CHAPTER 4

Reading and Printing

By now you should be able to do rather esoteric types of computations: but the way you get data into the computer and, more important, the form in which you get answers from the computer are still likely to cause you some embarrassment. This chapter will expand your ability to control such operations. Although you will not be able to do things as elegantly as a professional might, you will be able to use convenient forms of input and to produce readable output.

Data

As we have seen, you can think of data numbers as if they were in a list — when one data item is used (by a READ statement), an invisible pointer moves to the next one. To make this arrangement as vivid as possible, we have included just one number in each DATA statement. But this is not necessary at all. You may include as many numbers as you wish; just separate them with commas. The numbers will be used in order; that is, the first DATA statement (the one with the lowest line number) will be read from left to right, then the second, then the third, and so forth.

For example:

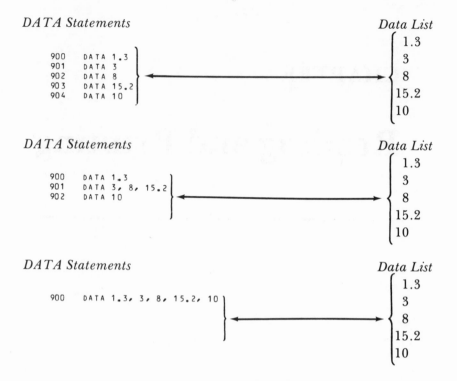

Obviously, the way in which the user writes any given set of numbers is primarily a matter of convenience. However they are written, the numbers will be used in the order of their appearance (reading each DATA statement from left to right and all DATA statements in order). Of course, only the ordering of numbers is relevant when the program goes to work.

DATA statements may be interspersed with program statements. However, to avoid confusion it is best to write them as a group after the last statement program.

The RESTORE Command

As we have seen, when a program is run, an invisible pointer is used to indicate the next data item to be read. At first it is set to point to the first (leftmost) data item in the lowest-numbered DATA statement. Every time an item is read, the pointer automatically moves right (within a DATA statement) or down (to the next DATA statement).

However, you can alter this automatic sequence. The command RESTORE resets the pointer to the first piece of data in the overall data list. This allows you to go through the list as many times as you want, without having to store all the data items in mailboxes so they will be available for later computations.

READ Commands

Recall the way we have been writing READ commands:

READ P

This means "Take the next number in the data list and put it in box P." To read two numbers in sequence we have said:

READ P
READ H

This is clearly a bother. The same thing can be accomplished by merely saying:

READ P, H

Would you like to read three values? Simply say:

READ X1, Y, Z9

This is precisely equivalent to:

READ X1
READ Y
READ Z9

You need only separate the names of the relevant variables with commas (so the computer will not get confused). Numbers from the data list will be put in the boxes indicated (from left to right).

Often it is useful to coordinate READ statements and DATA statements. You might choose to put each employee's data in a single DATA statement,

DATA 2.10, 41, 1, 2

and read it with the statement:

READ P, H, M, E

But remember that the correspondence is strictly for your benefit. Any equivalent arrangement of READ statements and/or DATA statements would give the same results.

Strings

A string is a sequence of characters enclosed in quotation marks. The characters may appear in any order and may be letters, digits, and/or any of the special symbols available in your system. Some examples of legal strings are:

> "HELLO"
> "1600 PENNSYLVANIA AVENUE"
> "MAY 31, 1970"
> "* (A) + − $"

A string may contain blanks anywhere. The only character a string may *not* contain is a quotation mark; the computer requires that you use quotations only to indicate where a string begins and ends.

Strings may be used to print a message as part of the output of a program. For example:

> PRINT "PAYROLL FOR JUNE, 1978"

The string will be printed *exactly* as you have written it, except that the quotation marks will not appear. (Note that blanks *do* count in strings, so put them in where you want them.)

There are other uses for strings in many BASIC systems. These will be discussed in chapter 9. For now, the real advantage of strings is that they allow us to label our numeric output so that the meaning of the numbers printed will be clear to anyone.

Skipping Lines

Output produced with BASIC is single-spaced. If you wish, however, you may tell the computer to skip a line. To do this, simply tell it to print nothing:

> PRINT

Printing the Values of Expressions

Thus far we have asked the computer to print only the values of variables. For example:

> PRINT P

But you may ask for the value of any legal expression:

> PRINT P
> PRINT 3.5
> PRINT A + 8
> PRINT (X * 3) ∧ 8

The expression will be evaluated; then the value (number) will be printed. The computer will decide the best way to print it. The number will be rounded to, say, six significant digits (ie., the leftmost digit that is not zero and the five digits to its right), and then printed in a reasonably attractive manner. If the number is extremely large or extremely small, the computer may be forced to print it as a decimal fraction followed by E and an appropriate power of ten. Of course, none of this affects the values of numbers in the computer (i.e., in the locations) — they remain in their original state.

Print Zones

Until now, we have printed only one number or one string per line. You may wish, however, to condense your output by printing several items on each line. No problem. The output sheet is divided into print zones for just that purpose. You need only specify the zones in which you want your output to appear (i.e., how you want the items spaced).

The output sheet is divided into *print zones.* There are generally five, with each one fifteen columns wide. The computer always starts a new line in the leftmost zone and works its way right. How are print zones used? Suppose you want to print four numbers on a line. You could tell the computer to:

PRINT P, H, M, E

This says: "Print the value of P (in the first zone), then space and print the value of H (in the second zone), then space and print the value of M (in the third zone), and finally, space and print the value of E (in the fourth zone)." Notice that the commas can be regarded as instructions to "space over to the next zone of fifteen columns."

What if the computer runs out of zones, as in:

PRINT P, H, M, E, X1, X2

The answer is obvious: X2 will be printed in the first zone on the next line.

Remember that you can ask the computer to print the value of any expression. For example, an entire payroll program might be written as follows:

```
10    READ P, H
20    PRINT P, H, P*H, .14*(P*H), .86*(P*H)
30    GO TO 10
```

You may also include strings. They are printed starting at the beginning of the next available zone. If a string is longer than the width of one zone, it will of course occupy two or more.

The output of the payroll program shown above could be improved by using strings:

```
 6    PRINT "PAY RATE","HOURS","GROSS","WITHHLDG","NET"
 7    PRINT
10    READ P, H
20    PRINT P, H, P*H, .14*(P*H), .86*(P*H)
30    GO TO 10
```

Here is how it will look (for the data values used in chapter 2):

```
PAY RATE       HOURS       GROSS       WITHHLDG       NET

  2.25          40           90         12.6          77.4
  3             41          123         17.22        105.78
  2.97          35          103.95      14.553        89.397
  3.1           49          151.9       21.266       130.634
```

You can, of course, print both strings and numeric values on the same line. For example:

$$\text{PRINT "PAY RATE} = \text{", P}$$

would produce this sort of output:

$$\text{PAY RATE} = \qquad 2.97$$

Notice that the comma itself is never printed. It serves only to tell the computer how to *space* the output. If you really want to print a comma for some reason, you'll simply have to print a string with one in it.

The Semicolon

The comma in a PRINT command allows you to print several items (usually five) per line. But you may want to print more. Or you may want several items more closely spaced than one per zone. What can you do? Use semicolons.

A semicolon tells the computer, in effect, "Don't move." To see how it works, let's look at the command:

$$\text{PRINT 13 ; 28.5;} - 18.6 ; 12$$

This would produce the following output:

$$13 \ 28.5 \ - 18.6 \ 12$$

Why don't the numbers simply run into one another? Because every positive number is automatically printed with one space before it (to its left) and one space after it (to its right). And every negative number is automatically printed with one space after it (to its right).

Here's a sample program using semicolons:

```
10    PRINT 1;2;3;4;5;6;7;8;9;10;11;12;13;14;15
20    PRINT 16;17;18;19;20;21;22;23;24;25;26;27
30    PRINT 28;29;30
```

Its output looks like this:

```
1     2     3     4     5     6     7     8     9     10    11
12    13    14    15
16    17    18    19    20    21    22    23    24    25    26
27
28    29    30
```

As always, if you give the computer too many items in a single PRINT command, it will start printing at the left of a new line when it runs out of space. This is helpful, because it may be difficult to anticipate the exact number of items that can be printed on a line.

Strings may also be printed using a semicolon. If you want to print two strings with no spaces between, you can. Or you can space them any way you want by adding blanks (inside the quotation marks, of course). Thus the command:

PRINT " THE PRESIDENT OF T";"HE UNITED STATES"

would result in the output:

THE PRESIDENT OF THE UNITED STATES

And the command:

PRINT "% ";"* ";"! ";"O ";"U ";"C ";"H "

would produce:

% * ! O U C H

As with the comma, you may print strings and expressions on the same line. And you may use both commas and semicolons in a single PRINT command. For example:

PRINT "PAY RATE = $";P," ","HOURS WORKED = ";H

would produce output like this:

PAY RATE = $ 2.97   HOURS WORKED = 35

Notice that a "blank" string (i.e., one with one or more blanks and nothing else) has been printed after the value of P. This is how "zone-skipping" is accomplished.

The rules for spacing may seem confusing. But don't let them bother you. Just remember that the semicolon can give you closer spacing than the comma. For many applications, the precise number of spaces between items is unimportant.

Dangling Commas and Semicolons

Normally, the output generated by a PRINT command is begun at the leftmost margin of a new line. There is one exception, however. It arises if the previously executed PRINT command ended with a comma or a semicolon. If it ended with a comma, the new output is started on the same line at the beginning of the next available zone. If it ended with a semicolon, the new output is started in the very next column.

Confusing? It's really very simple. To illustrate, the commands:

PRINT A; B;

PRINT C

produce exactly the same output as the single command:

PRINT A; B; C

As another example, the two programs below produce equivalent output.

Program A

```
10    READ P, H
20    LET G = P * H
30    LET W = .14 * G
40    LET N = G - W
50    PRINT P, H, G, W, N
60    GO TO 10
```

Program B

```
100   READ P, H
110   PRINT P, H,
120   LET G = P * H
130   PRINT G,
140   LET W = .14 * G
150   PRINT W,
160   LET N = G - W
170   PRINT N
180   GO TO 100
```

When might you want to use a dangling comma or semicolon? Perhaps you want to read in data items one at a time, but print them several to a line. For example:

```
10    READ A2
20    PRINT A2,
30    GO TO 10
```

The dangling comma tells the computer that the next print command *executed* should begin in the next zone. This holds even when the next print command executed is the same one (being executed again during a subsequent pass through the program). Therefore, the output of this program will contain five numbers on all but possibly the last line (depending on the number of data items).

Tab

A simple way to provide even more control over your output is to use a tab call with a PRINT command. For example:

TAB(20)

instructs the computer to "tab" over to the 20th column (from the left), as if it were a regular typewriter and you had pressed the "tab" key. In the normal case, the computer moves to the right (for example, from column 10 to column 20). If column 20 had alread been passed, the system would generally go to the next line, return to column 1, and then move to the right to column 20.[1]

Tab calls can be inserted at any place in a PRINT command; they are generally followed by semicolons to avoid further spacing. For example:

PRINT TAB(10); "FOTHERINGHAM"; TAB(25); "RANDOLPH"

would produce:

Tab calls are helpful when you want to produce neat lists with items lined up in columns.

---

1. Many systems that do not conform to the standards for Minimal BASIC would ignore the TAB in this instance.

Problems

1. Find any errors in the following statements:
   (a) PRINT "NUMBER EARNING "BREAD" REGULARLY"
   (b) PRINT A + B, C, "X = , X"
   (c) PRINT 3; 5.8; 9
   (d) READ A, B, C + D
   (e) READ A, B,
   (f) PRINT "ANNUAL PAY = $";25,300
2. Write a command that will print the word HELLO in the second zone.
3. Write a statement to print the letter X in the center of the first zone.
4. What output would be produced by the following program and data?

```
10    READ X, Y, Z
11    PRINT X, Y
12    PRINT Z
13    GO TO 10
900   REM -- DATA FOLLOW
901   DATA 3, 5.2, 8, 9
902   DATA 7, 10, 12
903   DATA 13, 15
999   END
```

5. What output would be produced by the following program?

```
50    LET I = 1
51    PRINT I,
52    IF I > 12 THEN 55
53    LET I = I + 1
54    GO TO 51
55    PRINT "    END"
56    STOP
99    END
```

6. What will the output of this program look like? (Don't bother to figure out the exact spacing between numbers.)

```
10    LET T = 0
15    READ A
20    PRINT A;
25    LET T = T + 1
30    IF T < 7 THEN 15
35    PRINT
40    GO TO 10
100   DATA 25, 32.8, 9
101   DATA 12.5, 17
102   DATA 1.24, 35, 101, 13.259
103   DATA 12.3, 30, 2
104   DATA 51, 93, 86.5, 7
199   END
```

7. What output would be produced by the following statement?

PRINT "NOW IS THE TIME"; TAB(10); "FOR ALL GOOD MEN"

Answers

1. (a) Strings may not include quotation marks. The reason is obvious. The computer would regard this as two strings — "NUMBER EARNING" and "REGULARLY" — with the word BREAD trapped between them.
   (b) The statement is legal. The value of A + B will be printed in the first zone; the value of C will be printed in the second zone, and the string:

   X = , X

   will be printed in the third zone. Perhaps this is what the programmer intended. More likely he or she meant:

   PRINT A + B, C, "X = ", X

   (c) This is perfectly legal because 3, 5.8 and 9 are all valid expressions (their values are, of course, 3, 5.8, and 9 respectively).
   (d) This is thoroughly illegal. You can read a number into box A and a second one into box B, but you cannot read a number into box C + D, because there is no such box. Numbers cannot be read into expressions; they can be read only into variables (boxes).
   (e) This is illegal. Commas are used to *separate* variable names in READ statements. The dangling comma is used *only* in PRINT statements.
   (f) This is legal, but the output may surprise the programmer. It will look like this:

   ANNUAL PAY = $ 25   300

   The reason is that the computer will interpret the comma as separating two numbers: 25 and 300. If the programmer intended to print a single number (25,300) with a comma in it, he should have said something like this:

   PRINT "ANNUAL PAY = $ 25,300"

   Commas may be embedded in a string, but *never* in a number.
2. This is an easy one. Just print a blank string in the first zone:

   PRINT " ", "HELLO"

3. Even easier. Just print seven blanks followed by X:

   PRINT "   X"

4.

```
    3     5.2
    8
    9     7
   10
   12     13
   15
```

5.

```
    1     2     3     4     5
    6     7     8     9    10
   11    12    13    END
```

6. The first seven values will be printed on line 1; the second seven on line 2. The remaining two numbers will appear on line 3. The PRINT statement in line 35 does not actually print a blank line—it simply serves to "clear" the dangling semicolon from the last item printed by line 20.

7.   column   column   column

                               1   10   16
                               ↓   ↓   ↓
                          NOW IS THE TIME
                                        .

                                        .

                                        .
                          FOR ALL GOOD MEN

After printing "NOW IS THE TIME," the computer was already in column 16. The only way for it to tab to column 10 was to space down to the next line, then move over to column 10 from column 1. This assumes you have a computer that would not ignore the TAB when it encounters this situation. (See footnote 1, this chapter.)

CHAPTER 5

Conversational Programming

In previous chapters we saw how the computer utilizes a BASIC program to operate on data. We always gave it data in the form of numbers included in DATA statements and then used READ statements to store the numbers in mailboxes so that other instructions could process them.

This method of supplying the computer with data requires that all the numbers be specified before the program is executed. Sometimes it may not be convenient, or even possible, to do so. For example, you might wish to see some of the program's results before selecting certain values to be input. You can do this by using the INPUT command to give the computer data during the execution of the program.

The INPUT Command

The READ command was an instruction to: "Take the next number from the data list and store it in the mailbox indicated." The INPUT command also stores data items in mailboxes; but instead of taking the items from the data list, it causes the computer to wait for you to type them in from your console. To see how it works, look at the following command:

100   INPUT Z6

When the computer encounters it, three things happen:

1. A character, usually a question mark ("?") is printed on the output sheet. This lets you know that the computer wants a data item.

2. Execution of the program is stopped until you are through. When you are, you signal the computer. In most systems the appropriate signal is a carriage return.
3. The number the computer receives from you is stored in variable Z6, and execution proceeds to the statement following line 100.

Thus when line 100 is reached, a question mark will appear on the output sheet:

?

You respond by typing a number:

?   53.57

The computer will wait for your signal and upon receiving it will store the number 53.57, in variable Z6 before continuing execution.

You may use input statements to enter data for any variable you wish. And you may enter data for more than one variable at a time. For example, the command:

INPUT   X4, S3, A0

will cause a question mark to be printed as before. But this time the computer will expect you to give it three numbers, separated by commas, before signaling it that you are done. Thus when the question mark appears, you might respond in the following way:

?   29.5, 67, 45.98

Just as with a DATA statement, the numbers are assigned to variables in the order that they appear from left to right. In this case 29.5 will be assigned to X4, 67 will be assigned to S3, and 45.98 will be assigned to A0.

Suppose you want to get some numbers from the data list and others from the console. No problem. Because input statements do not interfere with the data list, you are free to continue using READ and DATA statements just as before. Whenever you want a number from the data list, just use READ; whenever you want one from the console, use INPUT.

Using Print Statements with INPUT

It is helpful to include a PRINT statement before each INPUT statement in your program. Then you won't have to remember the order in which the program requires numbers; just let the PRINT statement refresh your memory. Here is an example:

```
50    PRINT "WHAT IS YOUR AGE ";
51    INPUT A
60    PRINT "AND YOUR WEIGHT ";
61    INPUT W
```

The output, after one person responded, looked like this:

```
WHAT IS YOUR AGE ? 21
AND YOUR WEIGHT ? 115
```

After line 50 was executed, the output was:

WHAT IS YOUR AGE

Upon reaching line 51, the computer printed a question mark:

WHAT IS YOUR AGE?

The response, 21, was typed in by the person:

WHAT IS YOUR AGE? 21

After storing the number in variable A, the computer proceeded to line 60. And so on.

But something strange happened when line 60 was encountered. The printing once again started at the left margin of a new line even though a dangling semicolon had been used in line 50. Why? In systems where the user signals the computer with a carriage return after typing his or her numbers, the computer will resume at the left margin automatically.

Printed instructions are also useful if you wish to have more than one number input at a time. Consider the following program segment:

```
100    PRINT "GIVE ME 2 NUMBERS --- AGE, WEIGHT"
101    INPUT A,W
```

Without line 100, you might forget that two numbers are required. If the wrong number of items is typed, various things can happen (depending on the system). The standard response is a request for you to start over and to supply the right number of items. In any event, it is a good idea to use print statements like this to increase the chances that the exact number of items will be input.

String Variables

Thus far we have dealt only with strings written out explicitly in a program. However, it is also possible to store strings. For this purpose a number of special mailboxes have been set aside to hold strings (just as the mailboxes previously discussed were set aside to hold numbers). These new mailboxes are called, logically, *string variables*. There are 26 of them. Each is named with a letter followed by a dollar sign: A$, B$, . . ., Z$. Standard systems provide enough space for each of these mailboxes to store a string of up to 18 characters.[1]

The use of string variables and input commands can greatly enhance your ability to make a program "converse" with a user, as we will see.

Use of Strings with LET and PRINT

A string variable may be assigned a value in a LET statement. Examples are:

> LET Z$ = "YES"
> LET R$ = A$

The first command assigns the three-character string "YES" to Z$. The second assigns a copy of the string in A$ to R$.

The string assigned to a string variable may contain any legal characters except embedded quotation marks. The following is perfectly legal:

> LET W$ = "123.65"

However, W$ will contain the six characters "123.65", *not* the numeric value 123.65. String variables cannot be used to hold numbers; thus it is illegal to say:

> LET W$ = 123.65

String variables may be printed:

> PRINT S$
> PRINT Y$; A$
> PRINT A, 47.5, "HELLO"; F$

The comma works the way it always has, and the semicolon gives you the same

1. Some systems provide more space, and some require that you indicate the amount of space needed via a DIM (dimension) statement similar to that described in chapter 7.

spacing as if the strings had been written explicitly.
Thus if A$ = "DATE − " and B$ = "DEC. 25, 1979", then:

PRINT A$;B$

would produce the output:

DATE − DEC. 25, 1979

As always, the quotation marks are not printed.

Reading and Inputting Strings

If you wish to read a string as data, just say:

READ A$

The corresponding data statement might look like this:

DATA "JOHN JONES"

More than one string may be read at a time, and string variables may be inter-
mixed with numeric variables in READ and DATA statements. Consider, for
example, the following revision of the payroll program.

Program

```
 5     PRINT "NAME", "PAY RATE", "GROSS PAY",
 7     PRINT "WITHHOLDING", "NET"
10     READ N$,P,H
20     PRINT N$, P, H, .14*(P*H), .86*(P*H)
30     GO TO 10
```

```
900    REM -- DATA FOR PAYROLL PROGRAM
901    DATA "JANE ADAMS", 2.25, 40
902    DATA "BOB CARTER", 3.00, 41
903    DATA "JOHN JONES", 2.97, 35
904    DATA "SAM MILLER", 3.10, 49
999    END
```

The rules the computer follows for ordering items in the data list are the
same as before. Just be sure to place the items in DATA statements so that
strings will be read into string variables and numbers will be read into
numeric variables.

Inputting strings is equally easy. Some examples of legal input statements and appropriate responses follow:

Statement	*Response*
INPUT C$	? "COLUMBUS"
INPUT E$, A1	? "SALES", 250
INPUT R, W$, Q$, P	? 35, "YES", "NO", 2.4

Not surprisingly, commas are used as separators between strings and numbers in responses.

When typing a string in response to an INPUT request, the user need not always type quotation marks. Everything from the leftmost (nonblank) character to the rightmost character in the input line will be considered part of the string.

Comparing Strings

Strings may be compared using IF statements. For example, the statement:

$$IF\ A\$ = "YES"\ THEN\ 100$$

causes the computer to transfer to line 100 if the string currently stored in A$ matches the string "YES".

The contents of two string variables might be compared by saying:

$$IF\ G\$ <> H\$\ THEN\ 450$$

Two strings are "equal" if they are exact copies of each other. Otherwise, they are "unequal." Thus "123.65" and 123.650" are not equal; neither are " SMITH" and "SMITH".[2] (Remember blanks are important in strings.)

An Application

Input commands enable you (or someone else) to decide whether to go to one part of your program or to another, depending on the situation. This allows the user to carry on a "conversation" with your program. In fact, it is possible to write a program that can be used effectively by someone who knows nothing about programming, DATA statements, etc. Here is a simple example:

2. In some systems not conforming to the standards for Minimal BASIC, blanks occurring at the rightmost end of the strings being compared are ignored. In such systems, "YES " is equal to "YES." See chapter 9 for further discussion.

```
100    REM -- PROGRAM FOR MATH TEST
110    PRINT "WHAT IS YOUR NAME";
111    INPUT N$
120    PRINT
130    PRINT "A NUMBER PLEASE";
131    INPUT N1
140    PRINT "AND ANOTHER";
141    INPUT N2
150    PRINT "WHAT IS ";N1;" + ";N2;
151    INPUT A
160    REM --------------------
161    REM -- SEE IF ANSWER IS CORRECT
162    IF A = (N1+N2) THEN 200
170    REM ---------- WRONG ANSWER
171    PRINT "SORRY -- WRONG ANSWER. WANT TO TRY AGAIN";
172    INPUT A$
173    IF A$ = "YES" THEN 150
175    GOTO 210
200    REM ---------- RIGHT ANSWER
201    PRINT "GOOD FOR YOU, ";N$
210    PRINT
211    PRINT "WANT TO TRY ANOTHER PROBLEM";
212    INPUT A$
214    IF A$ = "YES" THEN 120
300    REM ---------- ALL THROUGH
301    PRINT "O.K. ";N$;" -- GOODBYE"
999    END
```

Here is an example of a "conversation" with this program. To make its operation clearer, the portions typed by the user have been underlined.

```
WHAT IS YOUR NAME?DEBBIE

A NUMBER PLEASE?2
AND ANOTHER?4
WHAT IS 2     + 4     ?7
SORRY -- WRONG ANSWER. WANT TO TRY AGAIN?YES
WHAT IS 2     + 4     ?6
GOOD FOR YOU, DEBBIE

WANT TO TRY ANOTHER PROBLEM?YES

A NUMBER PLEASE?245
AND ANOTHER?163
WHAT IS 245   + 163   ?408
GOOD FOR YOU, DEBBIE

WANT TO TRY ANOTHER PROBLEM?NO
O.K. DEBBIE -- GOODBYE
```

As you can see, a little effort on the part of the programmer can make a user consider "the computer" downright friendly.

Problems

1. What, if anything, is wrong with the following responses to input commands? Assume that in every case the program wants one number.

(a) HOW MANY CHILDREN DO YOU HAVE ? I HAVE 3.

(b) WHAT IS YOUR ANNUAL INCOME ? 7,000

(c) HOW MANY INCHES IN A FOOT ? 25.30

(d) A PINT IS WHAT PORTION OF A QUART ? 1/2

2. Assume you work for a small market research firm. You have been asked to interview local citizens regarding their television viewing habits. Among the questions you must ask each interviewee are the following:

(a) Do you own a television?

(b) If not, do you contemplate buying one in the next year?

(c) If yes, do you watch it during the daytime

   (1) often

   (2) seldom

   (3) never

Write a program to ask these questions.

Answers

1. (a) "I HAVE 3" is not a number.

   (b) The user gave the program too many numbers.

   (c) This is perfectly acceptable. The computer looks only to see if the number is a legal constant.

   (d) 1/2 is an expression, not a legal constant. Expressions may not be used as data items, either in data statements or as responses to input commands. The user should have typed the fraction in decimal form: e.g., as 0.5.

2. Your program might look something like this:

```
10    REM -- INTERVIEWING PROGRAM: TELEVISION
11    REM -- VIEWING HABITS
15    PRINT "HELLO.  I WOULD LIKE TO ASK YOU SOME"
16    PRINT "QUESTIONS ABOUT YOUR T.V. VIEWING."
17    PRINT
18    PRINT "IF YOU OWN A TELEVISION, PLEASE TYPE"
19    PRINT "A 1.  IF YOU DONT, TYPE 0";
20    INPUT A1
30    IF A1 = 1 THEN 50
40    PRINT "IF YOU PLAN TO BUY ONE IN THE NEXT YEAR"
41    PRINT "TYPE A 1.  IF NOT, TYPE 0 ";
42    INPUT A2
43    GO TO 60
50    PRINT "DO YOU WATCH YOUR TELEVISION DURING THE"
51    PRINT "DAYTIME:"
52    PRINT "  1  OFTEN"
53    PRINT "  2  SELDOM"
54    PRINT "  3  NEVER"
55    PRINT "TYPE A 1, 2, OR 3 ";
56    INPUT A3
60    PRINT
62    PRINT "THANK YOU."
63    STOP
```

CHAPTER 6

Loops

One of the most useful techniques in programming involves the *loop*—the repeated execution of a series of statements with one or more changes made each time. Several loops have already been written; most programs contain so many that it is desirable to be able to write them succinctly. This chapter describes the FOR and NEXT commands. They allow you to replace several statements with two and, equally important, to make the structure of a loop much more obvious to anyone reading your program (including you).

FOR and NEXT

It is obviously senseless to repeat a series of statements unless something changes each time. Usually (but not always) the thing that changes is the value of some variable. In the typical case the variable is set at some *initial value*, and the relevant statements executed. Then the variable is changed (*stepped*) by some amount (up or down) and the statements executed again. Eventually, the variable will pass some desired *terminal value*; at this point the computer is expected to proceed with the remainder of the program.

Assume that you want to compute and print the present value of a dollar at an interest rate of 5 percent under various assumptions concerning the year in which the dollar becomes available. If it turns up in year N, the present value is

$$P = 1/(1.05 \wedge N)$$

55

The following loop would compute and print the desired values for years 1 through 25:

```
10   LET N = 1
15   REM
20   LET P = 1 / (1.05^N)
21   PRINT "   YEAR   "; N
22   PRINT "PRESENT VALUE ="; P
23   PRINT
25   REM
30   IF N >= 25 THEN 40
31   LET N = N + 1
32   GO TO 20
35   REM
40   STOP
45   END
```

In this case the variable that changes as the loop is executed over and over is N; its initial value is 1, its terminal value is 25, and the step is 1. Statements 10, 30, 31, and 32 take care of the housekeeping required to perform the operations in the desired manner. The loop itself consists of statements 20 through 25. When the looping is finished, the computer is supposed to go to statement 40 (which is the end of the program in this case).

A simpler way to write the program is as follows:[1]

```
10   FOR N = 1 TO 25 STEP 1
20     LET P = 1 / (1.05 ^ N)
21       PRINT "   YEAR   "; N
22       PRINT "PRESENT VALUE ="; P
23       PRINT
30   NEXT N
35   REM
40   STOP
```

Not only are there fewer statements (two statements have replaced four), but the key information is contained in one statement (number 10), where it is more obvious to the reader (and to the programmer).

The statements comprising a loop written in this manner fall between the FOR statement and its associated NEXT statement. The variable to be altered when the loop is repeated is indicated in both statements, immediately after the command FOR and again after NEXT. The initial, terminal, and step values are indicated in that order in the FOR statement. The general form is:

FOR *variable = initial value* TO *terminal value* STEP *step value*

---

1. For clarity, statements within loops will sometimes be indented here. Some computers preserve such indentations; others do not.

Any or all of the three values may be indicated by expressions:

$$\text{FOR } X = A + B \text{ TO } 3 * X \text{ STEP } N$$

The STEP may be omitted; it will then be assumed to be one:

$$\text{FOR } Z = 1 \text{ TO } 25$$

What does the computer do when it encounters a FOR statement? First, it sets the variable to the indicated initial value. Then it tests to see if it is already past the indicated terminal value; if so, it immediately transfers to the statement following the associated NEXT command. If not, the statements in the loop are executed. When the NEXT command is encountered, the computer adds (algebraically) the step value to the current value of the variable and tests again to see if it has passed the terminal value. If so, it goes on to the statements following the NEXT statement. If not, it goes back to the statement following the FOR statement. The process continues as long as necessary.

We have said (rather vaguely) that looping is terminated when the variable "passes" the specified terminal value. Just what does this mean? The answer is that it depends on the step being used. If the step size is positive, it means that the variable *exceeds* the terminal value (since the loop involves increasing values of the variable). If the step size is negative, it means that the variable is *smaller* (algebraically) than the terminal value (since the loop involves decreasing values of the variable). Needless to say, the step size should never be zero; this would imply that you wanted the computer to loop forever.

It is a good idea to avoid altering any variables mentioned in the FOR statement while you are in the loop. You may, if you wish, transfer out of a loop (with an IF or GO TO command). But you should avoid any subsequent transfer back into the middle of the loop.[2]

Loops may be nested inside each other. For example:

$$\text{FOR } I = 1 \text{ TO } 10$$
$$\text{FOR } J = 1 \text{ TO } 10$$
$$\bullet$$
$$\bullet$$
$$\bullet$$
$$\text{NEXT } J$$
$$\text{NEXT } I$$

They may *not* "cross" as in the following example:

---

2. A formal exception occurs when a subroutine (described in chapter 9) transfers back to a loop from which it was called.

$$\begin{aligned}&\text{FOR I} = 1 \text{ TO } 10\\&\quad\text{FOR J} = 1 \text{ TO } 10\\&\text{NEXT I}\\&\quad\text{NEXT J}\end{aligned}$$

All this may sound as if FOR-NEXT statements are more bother than they are worth. But in most cases you will find that they work quite nicely if you simply do what seems natural. The details indicated above to avoid possible problems are relevant only for cases in which a programmer attempts something exotic.

Examples

A few examples may be helpful. First, assume that you want to produce a table showing the present value of a dollar at 1, 2, 3, and 4 percent when the dollar becomes available in years 1 through 25. One way of doing this is as follows:

```
10    REM -- HEAD TABLE
12    PRINT "        PRESENT VALUE OF A DOLLAR"
13    PRINT
14    PRINT "YEAR","1 PCNT","2 PCNT","3 PCNT","4 PCNT"
15    PRINT
17    REM
19    REM -- COMPUTE AND PRINT VALUES
20    FOR N = 1 TO 25
21       LET P1 = 1 / (1.01^N)
22       LET P2 = 1 / (1.02^N)
23       LET P3 = 1 / (1.03^N)
24       LET P4 = 1 / (1.04^N)
25       PRINT N, P1, P2, P3, P4
26       PRINT
27    NEXT N
28    REM
30    STOP
40    END
```

A slightly more compact way of writing it is the following:

```
10    REM -- HEAD TABLE
12    PRINT "        PRESENT VALUE OF A DOLLAR"
13    PRINT
14    PRINT "YEAR","1 PCNT","2 PCNT","3 PCNT","4 PCNT"
15    PRINT
18    REM
19    REM -- COMPUTE AND PRINT VALUES
20    FOR N = 1 TO 25
21       PRINT N,
22       FOR R = .01 TO .04 STEP .01
23          PRINT 1/((1+R)^N) ,
24       NEXT R
25       PRINT
26    NEXT N
28    REM
30    STOP
40    END
```

In this simple approach, the inner loop spins R from .01 through .04 for each value of N from 1 to 25. Never again need you stand in awe of those massive tables of interest calculations found in so many reference books.

The next example illustrates the use of a loop to decrease the value of a variable. Assume that you want to read a number (call it N) and compute its factorial (F). The factorial of a number is found by multiplying it by itself less one, then by itself less two, and the like, until you get to one. In other words:

$$F = N * (N - 1) * (N - 2) * \ldots * 1$$

Now study the following program:

```
10    REM -- READ NUMBER, COMPUTE AND PRINT FACTORIAL
11    READ N
12    LET F = N
13    FOR M = N-1 TO 1 STEP -1
14      LET F = F * M
15    NEXT M
16    PRINT "FACTORIAL OF "; N; "= "; F
17    GO TO 11
20    END
```

See how it works? If not, play computer and follow the instructions with a number or two.

The final example is rather trivial. Assume that you want to skip five lines on the output sheet:

```
FOR K = 1 TO 5
  PRINT
NEXT K
```

Admittedly, the variable (K) is not used at all inside the loop. But who said that it had to be?

FOR-NEXT loops are extremely helpful when dealing with lists and tables. But that discussion must be deferred until the next chapter.

Problems

1. Find any logical errors in the following program segment (part of a program):

```
10    FOR Z = 1 TO 30
11      IF Z = 5 THEN 10
12      PRINT Z
13    NEXT Z
```

2. Find any logical errors in the following program segment:

```
10    FOR Z = 1 TO 25 STEP -1
11       PRINT Z
12    NEXT Z
```

3. Write a program to calculate and print the squares of the odd integers (whole numbers) from 1 to some number N. Arrange to have the value of N read in as data.

4. Write a program to compute the factorials of the numbers 1 through 10.

5. What output will be produced by the following program segment?

```
10    FOR N = 1 TO 5
15       FOR I = 1 TO N-1 STEP 1
20          PRINT " ",
25       NEXT I
30       FOR I = 1 TO 6-N STEP 1
35          PRINT I,
40       NEXT I
45    NEXT N
```

6. Write a program using the FOR and NEXT commands rather extensively. Keep at it until you are convinced that you understand how to use them.

7. Most computers do their calculations with binary numbers (i.e., numbers to the base two, involving only zeros and ones). This can sometimes cause a problem when summing fractions. What kind of problem might arise, and how can it be solved?

Answers

1. The first time through the loop, Z will equal 1; the condition in statement 11 will not be met and Z will be printed. So far, so good. The second time through, Z will be 2. Again, no problem. The difficulty will arise during the fifth time through: Z will equal 5 and the condition in statement 11 *will* be met. The computer will then transfer back to the FOR statement and start all over again. This portion of the program will thus try to produce an infinite set of output consisting of the numbers 1, 2, 3, 4, 1, 2, 3, 4, 1, 2, ... Presumably, the programmer meant to have the computer avoid printing Z when it is 5. If so, he or she should have told it go to the NEXT statement:

11   IF Z = 5 THEN 13

2. The step size here is negative. That means that the loop will be terminated as soon as the variable falls *below* 25. But its initial value (1) is already below 25. Thus the statement inside the loop (number 11) will never be executed.

3. Here is a possibility:

```
100    READ N
110    FOR I = 1 TO N STEP 2
120       PRINT "THE SQUARE OF "; I; " IS "; I^2
130    NEXT I
135    REM
140    STOP
900    REMARK -- DATA
901    DATA 15
999    END
```

4. Simply modify the example shown earlier:

```
10    FOR N = 1 TO 10
12       LET F = N
13       FOR M = N-1 TO 1 STEP -1
14          LET F = F * M
15       NEXT M
16       PRINT "FACTORIAL OF "; N; "= "; F
17    NEXT N
20    STOP
30    END
```

Note that this program requires no data (no problem: just give it none).

5. This one requires some concentration. The output looks like this:

```
1     2     3     4     5
      1     2     3     4
            1     2     3
                  1     2
                        1
```

If you didn't get this correct, play computer and go through the program again very carefully. Watch the FOR-NEXT loop in lines 15 to 25 particularly closely; when N equals 1, it doesn't get executed at all.

6. Never minimize the importance of writing actual programs and getting them to work correctly. It is the best way to learn programming.

7. Such complications rarely occur, but they can be irritating. The problem is the computer's inability to represent certain fractions with perfect accuracy as binary numbers (including some that can be easily represented as decimal fractions). Summing a number of such fractions may thus give a smaller total than expected. This should not be surprising, since it arises even with a desk calculator. For example:

$$1/3 + 1/3 + 1/3$$
$$= .33333333 + .33333333 + .33333333$$
$$+ .99999999$$

which is slightly less than 1.

The solution is simply to anticipate the possibility. For example, instead of saying:

$$IF\ T = 1\ THEN\ 100$$

say:

$$IF\ T >= .999999\ THEN\ 100$$

Note, however, that this kind of problem can occur only with fractions (and only with certain fractions at that). By and large, you need not worry about it.

CHAPTER 7

Lists and Tables

By now you should realize that it is possible to store many different numbers simultaneously. You simply put them into different boxes (i.e., give them different variable names). Numbers can be put into a box with a READ statement or a LET statement. And once a number is in a box it can be referenced in any expression (e.g., in a LET, PRINT, or IF statement). But there is one problem that has undoubtedly plagued you already: If a group of numbers is to be stored concurrently, each must have a different name (i.e., be in a different box). And the number of names is rather limited.

To overcome this difficulty and to allow more powerful techniques to be employed, programmers make extensive use of *lists* and *tables*. The general notion is simple. Imagine that you want to read and store the prices of eleven different products. You could say:

READ   P1, P2, P3, P4, P5, P6, P7, P8, P9, R1, R2

But it would be much simpler if you could use a single letter to represent the type of information (e.g., P for price) and then refer to the prices as P(1), P(2), ... Continuing with the analogy of mailboxes, you would refer to a box by its street (P) and the number on the street. Thus P(3) would refer to box 3 on P street, and P(11) to box 11 on P street. More relevant for our purposes, P(3) would refer to the third item in *list* P, P(11) to the eleventh item, and so forth. The use of such lists will greatly expand the range of problems that you can program easily. And the use of tables will expand it even further.

Lists

You may arbitrarily decide to use any letter for the name of a list.[1] The particular item in the list is indicated within parentheses immediately following the name of the list. Thus:

> A(3) is the third item in list A
> Z(97) is the ninety-seventh item in list Z

Remember that a letter followed by a digit may *not* be used for the name of a list (or table, for that matter). Thus A9(3), for example, is quite illegal. Moreover, once you have appropriated a letter to serve as the name of a list or table, you should not use it for anything else.

How many items may there be in each list? Unless you tell it otherwise, the computer will make provisions for ten. How does it know that you have decided to use a particular letter for the name of a list? It looks over your program before going to work; if it sees a letter followed by parentheses, it figures out what you are up to and acts accordingly.

You may refer to the number in a particular box in a list by giving the item number explicitly:

> A(3)
> A(65)

or implicitly, using any legal expression:

> A(Z)
> B(Q3)
> C(A + (B * D))

When the item number is indicated implicitly, the computer:

1. Evaluates the expression inside the parentheses.
2. Rounds the result to the nearest integer (whole number).
3. Uses the appropriate item in the list.

It is imperative that you understand this procedure perfectly. For example, there is no such thing as A(I) or A(J); there is an item in box A(1), another in box A(2), and so on. Whenever the computer encounters A(I) during the execution of the program, it looks at the current value of I, substitutes it, and then finds the desired item in list A. To state it another way, when you refer to box A(I) in your program you are referring to an item in list A whose item

---

1. Don't confuse *lists* (described here) with the *data list* (described earlier). The *data list* is made up automatically from the items in DATA statements. *Lists* are created and used by your program, in ways that you choose.

number (position in the list) is stored in mailbox I. The following example illustrates the procedure.

Assume that at the moment:

$$I = 2$$
$$J = 4$$
$$K = 6$$

Then:

A(I) refers to A(2) — the second item in list A
A(J) refers to A(4) — the fourth item in list A
A(K) refers to A(6) — the sixth item in list A
A(I + J) refers to A(6) — the sixth item in list A

You may refer (explicitly or implicitly) to any item number in the list in question for which space has been reserved (of course you need not use all the reserved spaces). If you ever attempt to refer to an item for which space has not been reserved (e.g., a negative item number or one exceeding the space reserved), the computer will complain.

The idea of a list is very similar to the notion of a subscripted variable used in mathematics. Thus the mathematician might write X_3 to indicate the value of the third of a series of variables named X. We would write this as X(3). For this reason we often call lists (and tables, too, for that matter) *subscripted variables.* Regular variables are thus *unsubscripted variables*, and they are quite different. Notice, for example, the difference between the unsubscripted variable P3 (the mailbox named P3) and the subscripted variable P(3) — the third item in list P.

Standard systems have an additional feature that can prove useful for mathematical procedures: they reserve boxes for a zero'th item in each list. If you wish, you can instruct them not to do this by including the command:

OPTION BASE 1

prior to any references to subscripted variables.

Unless you are especially intrigued by the notion of a zero'th item in a list, the best approach is simply to assume that all lists begin with item 1. Then, if your computer wishes to reserve space for a zero'th item, let it do so — it won't bother you one way or the other.

Reading Data into a List

Assume that you want to read twenty-five numbers into a list named X. Now the FOR statement really comes into its own:

```
10    FOR I = 1 TO 25
11      READ X(I)
12    NEXT I
```

The first time through the loop I equals 1. When statement 11 is executed, the computer reads a number from the data stack into box X(1)—the first box in list X. The second time through, I equals 2; the number is thus read into X(2)—the second box in the list. And so it goes, until all twenty-five numbers have been placed in their appropriate boxes.

Perhaps you want to read thirty pairs of numbers into lists X and Y; the first pair into X(1) and Y(1), the second pair into X(2) and Y(2), and so forth. This presents no problem:

```
10    FOR I = 1 TO 30
11      READ X(I), Y(I)
12    NEXT I
```

As a final example, assume that the first number in the data list tells how many pairs are to be read. Then you simply write the following:

```
 9    READ N
10    FOR I = 1 TO N
11      READ X(I), Y(I)
12    NEXT I
```

Sorting Data

An important operation with lists involves sorting data into either increasing or decreasing order. There are many ways of doing this; we will use one of the least efficient (but most easily understood).

Assume there are thirty numbers in list X and you want to rearrange them so they will be in order, with the largest number first and the smallest last. The trick is to compare pairs of adjacent numbers. If the first one is larger than the second (or equal to it), the pair is acceptable. If not, the numbers should be switched. Obviously if all pairs are acceptable, the list is in the desired order. If not, it may or may not be. We thus want to pass through the list comparing all the adjacent pairs of numbers and recording the number of switches made. After completing a pass through the list, we check the number of switches. If none was made, the sorting is complete. If some pairs had to be switched, however, we pass through the list again to see if more switches are required. An example follows:

```
10    LET S = 0
11    FOR I = 1 TO 29
12       IF X(I) >= X(I+1) THEN 17
13       LET S = S + 1
14       LET Z = X(I)
15       LET X(I) = X(I+1)
16       LET X(I+1) = Z
17    NEXT I
18    IF S > 0 THEN 10
19    REM -- PROCEED
```

Note the way in which the switch is made. The number currently in box X(I) is stored temporarily in box Z. Then the number currently in box X(I + 1) is placed in box X(I). Finally, the number in box Z is placed in box X(I + 1). To see why all this is necessary, assume that:

$$I = 8$$
$$X(8) = 12$$
$$X(9) = 15$$

Now follow these instructions:

$$\text{LET } X(I) = X(I + 1)$$
$$\text{LET } X(I + 1) = X(I)$$

Obviously this would have disastrous results.

Note also that the FOR statement instructs the computer to let I = 1, 2, . . . 29. Why not let I equal 30? Because this would cause a comparison between X(30) and X(31); and we want to sort only the first 30 numbers in list X.

What would happen if the comparison had been written as:

$$12 \quad \text{IF } X(I) > X(I + 1) \text{ THEN 17}$$

Nothing, fortunately, if no two numbers were equal; but had there been at least one pair of numbers with the same value, the process could have continued indefinitely.

Finally, consider a problem in which you want to sort the values in increasing order. Just change the comparison to:

$$12 \quad \text{IF } X(I) <= X(I + 1) \text{ THEN 17}$$

Enough about sorting. It must be done with care, but it can be very useful.

Printing Numbers from a List

Assume that you would like to print the first N numbers from list X in a single column (i.e., one number per line). Just write the following:

```
10    FOR I = 1 TO N
11       PRINT X(I)
12    NEXT I
```

If you would prefer to have the numbers printed in all the zones (i.e., from left to right on line 1, then on line 2, and so on), just add a comma:

```
10    FOR I = 1 TO N
11       PRINT X(I),
12    NEXT I
```

Recall that the dangling comma tells the computer that the next print command executed should begin in the next available zone. Therefore, after the looping is completed it is a good idea to "clear" the system; otherwise the next print command (located somewhere else in the program) may begin its output in the middle of the page (i.e., in the next available zone). The simplest way to accomplish this is to give the command PRINT after printing the numbers from the list:

```
10    FOR I = 1 TO N
11       PRINT X(I),
12    NEXT I
13    PRINT
```

This approach could also have been employed if a dangling semicolon had been used in line 11.

Of course, there are many ways to print data contained in lists. Here is one last example:

```
10    PRINT "LIST P"
15    PRINT
20    FOR I = 1 TO M
25       PRINT "P(";I;") ="; P(I)
30    NEXT I
```

The output will look something like this:

```
LIST P

P( 1      ) = 37.4
P( 2      ) = 89.55
P( 3      ) =-12.2
```

Finding the Largest Number in a List

We can illustrate the points made thus far with a simple program designed to read a set of prices and to find the largest one. We assume that the first data number indicates the number of prices and that each price is followed by an identifying item number. The program is designed to find the largest price, then print it and the item numbers of all items with that price (there may be more than one).

The technique is relatively straightforward. Initially, the price of the first item is taken as the (temporary) maximum. Each price is then compared with the (current) maximum. If the new price is equal or smaller, no change is made; but if the new price is greater, it becomes the new (temporary) maximum. When all prices have been processed, the temporary maximum is clearly the real maximum. A second pass through the data is used to find the item numbers with that price. The program follows:

```
10      READ N
12      REM -- READ IN LISTS P AND I
20      FOR K = 1 TO N
21         READ P(K), I(K)
22      NEXT K
25      REM -- LOOK FOR MAXIMUM
30      LET M = P(1)
31      FOR K = 2 TO N
32         IF P(K) <= M THEN 34
33         LET M = P(K)
34      NEXT K
37      REM -- PRINT RESULTS
40      PRINT "MAXIMUM PRICE IS "; M
41      PRINT "ITEM NUMBERS FOLLOW "
50      FOR K=1 TO N
51         IF P(K) <> M THEN 53
52         PRINT I(K);
53      NEXT K
54      PRINT
60      STOP
```

Obviously, the *smallest* price (and associated item numbers) could have been found if the comparison had been written as:

$$32 \quad \text{IF } P(K) >= M \text{ THEN } 34$$

Tables

Lists are very useful, but for some problems they are not enough. For example, you might be interested in ten cities. You could easily use lists to refer to the altitudes of the cities (e.g., $A(1), A(2)$, and the like) or to their populations (e.g., P(1), P(2), and the like), but you might also want to refer to the distances between pairs of cities. For this you would need a *table* — one probably named D. The number in the third row and fifth column (showing the distance between city 3 and city 5) could be described most simply as:

$$D(3,5)$$

And that is exactly how it would be described. You may appropriate any (single) letter to represent the name of a table. The particular item in the table is indicated in parentheses, with the row number first and the column number second. The row and column numbers must be separated by a comma. Either or both may be indicated implicitly, using any legal expression:

$$D(3,5)$$
$$D(I,5)$$
$$D(I,J)$$
$$D(A + B,8)$$
$$D(3, X/Y)$$
$$D(A + B, X(I))$$

When an implicit row or column number is given, the computer evaluates the expression and then rounds the result to the nearest integer to determine the relevant row and/or column in the table. Both row and column number are checked to insure that space has been reserved for the item in question. If you do not explicitly reserve space, the computer will provide enough for you to use row numbers as great as 10 and column numbers as great as 10.

Standard systems provide for a zero'th row and a zero'th column in tables, but this can be avoided by using the OPTION BASE 1 command. Alternatively, the whole issue can be ignored (as with lists); simply assume that all tables start with row 1 and column 1 and you need not worry, no matter what computer system you use.

How does the computer know that you have decided to use a letter for a table? By looking over your program. If it finds a letter followed by a set of parentheses with a comma inside, it isn't very difficult to guess what you have in mind. But be consistent — if you decide to use a letter for a table name, do not use it for the name of a list (and vice versa).[2]

2. In general, a letter should not be used for more than one of the following purposes: (1) a list name; (2) a table name; and (3) a simple (unsubscripted) variable name. Thus, if Z is used for the name of a list, there should be no table named Z and no use of the regular mailbox Z. Use of mailboxes with two-character names starting with Z (e.g., Z1, Z$) would, however, be perfectly acceptable.

Reading Data into a Table

To take a simple example first, let's suppose you want to set up a 3-row, 2-column table in your program, and you have prepared the entries for the table in DATA statements:

```
900    DATA 2.5, 33
901    DATA 19, 27
902    DATA 12.7, 5
```

The numbers are arranged so that each DATA statement represents one row in the table; statement 900 contains the entries for row 1, statement 901 contains the entries for row 2, and so on. The leftmost number in each statement goes in column 1 of the appropriate row; the rightmost number goes in column 2. How can we get all the numbers from the data list into their respective places in the table?

It's easy. Let us first adopt some conventions. The name of the table will be R, and we will use the letters I and J to refer to a particular row and column, respectively, in the table. The following set of instructions reads in the first row of R:

```
10    LET I = 1
20    FOR J = 1 TO 2
30    READ R(I,J)
40    NEXT J
```

The first time through the loop, J equals 1, and the number 2.5 is read into R(1,1). The second time through J equals 2, and the number 33 is read into R(1,2). But what about rows 2 and 3? We'd like to do the same thing over again with I reset to 2 and then, finally, with I reset to 3. By now, you have probably guessed what's coming next: another FOR loop, this one varying I from 1 to 3. The complete set of instructions to read in the table looks like this:

```
10    FOR I = 1 TO 3
20      FOR J = 1 TO 2
30        READ R(I,J)
40      NEXT J
50    NEXT I
```

And by modifying the terminal values in statements 10 and 20, you can read in any size table you want (provided sufficient space has been reserved).

One more example. Assume that you want to set up a table of distances for ten cities. Each set of three data numbers describes a direct route between two cities. For example:

900   DATA 3,5,275

indicates that there is a route connecting cities 3 and 5 and that the distance is 275 miles. In the table the number 275 should thus be entered in row 3, column 5, and also in row 5, column 3.

What about the distance from a city to itself? It is obviously zero. Thus D(1,1) should be set to zero, as should D(2,2), D(3,3), and so on. What about cities not connected directly? We want the table to show a very long distance (9999 miles, to be specific) for such cases.

The instructions required to set up the table are relatively simple. First all entries are set to 9999, except those along the diagonal (D(1,1),D(2,2),D(3,3), and so forth), which are set to zero. Then sets of data are read and the distances entered in the appropriate positions in the table (throwing out the previously entered values of 9999). The final set of data is assumed to consist of negative numbers, signaling the end of this phase of the problem.

The program segment follows:

```
10    REM -- SET UP 9999 VALUES AND ZEROES ON DIAGONAL
20    FOR I = 1 TO 10
30      FOR J = 1 TO 10
31        IF I = J THEN 35
32        REM -- THIS IS NOT ALONG THE DIAGONAL
33        LET D(I,J) = 9999
34        GO TO 37
35        REM -- THIS IS ALONG THE DIAGONAL
36        LET D(I,J) = 0
37      NEXT J
39    NEXT I
40    REM -- READ A SET OF DATA
41      READ C1, C2, M
42    REM -- TEST FOR A NEGATIVE NUMBER
43      IF C1 < 0 THEN 50
44    REM -- ENTER DISTANCE
45      LET D(C1,C2) = M
46      LET D(C2,C1) = M
47    REM -- GO BACK TO READ ANOTHER SET OF DATA
48      GO TO 40
50    REM -- PROCEED
```

If you find this difficult to understand, remember the advice given earlier: play computer. If a machine can understand these instructions, why not you?

Using Tables

The concept of a subscripted variable is actually quite simple. To understand it *perfectly* requires some diligence, but the effort is worth it. Once you have mastered subscripted variables, you will be able to write quite sophisticated programs using lists and tables. There are literally hundreds of applications. One is described below; you will, undoubtedly, think of others.

The example comes from security analysis. The data are the closing prices of shares of common stock on the last day of each of several months. Pick any ten stocks, then look up their prices for the last day of each of the past six months. You would then have sixty data values, one for each stock on the last day of a particular month. The values will be read into a table named S. The row in S of any item will be its stock number, and the column in S will be the month. Thus, S(4,6) refers to the price of stock 4 on the last day of month 6. Obviously, there will be ten rows and six columns in S.

We have selected common stocks and considered only sixty data values. But we could pick anything whose price or magnitude varies from time to time, use any time interval we wish, and have almost any number of values (within reason). The program should work just as well if we use the number of fish caught daily in each of five lakes during a one-week period. We would have to change only the number of rows and columns in S.

But back to stocks. Let's assume we're interested in knowing the following things about the data in S:

1. The average price (over the six monthly values) for each stock.
2. The standard deviation of the prices for each stock.[3]
3. The average price (over all stocks) for each month.

Here's the program:

```
10    REM --- SECURITY ANALYSIS PROGRAM
11    REM
12    REM -- SET UP NUMBER OF ROWS, COLUMNS IN S
15      LET N = 10
16      LET M = 6
```

3. Standard deviation is the square root of the average squared deviations from the mean (i.e., average) of a series of numbers. It will give an idea of the extent to which actual prices differed from the average price. If the standard deviation is very large, price varied quite a bit from month to month. If the standard deviation is close to zero, price remained fairly constant.

```
17     REM
20     REM -- READ IN TABLE
21     FOR I = 1 TO N
22       FOR J = 1 TO M
23         READ S(I,J)
24       NEXT J
25     NEXT I
27     REM
30     REM -- PRINT HEADINGS
35     PRINT "SECURITY", "AVERAGE PRICE", "STD DEVIATION"
37     PRINT
38     REM
40     REM -- FIND AVERAGE PRICE, STD DEVIATION
42     REM -- FOR EACH STOCK
50     FOR I = 1 TO N
52       LET T1 = 0
55       FOR J = 1 TO M
57         LET T1 = T1 + S(I,J)
60       NEXT J
62       LET A = T1/M
63       LET T2 = 0
65       FOR J = 1 TO M
67         LET T2 = T2 + (S(I,J) - A)^2
70       NEXT J
72       LET D = (T2/M)^.5
74       PRINT I, A, D
80     NEXT I
82     PRINT
84     PRINT
86     REM
90     REM -- PRINT HEADINGS
92     PRINT "MONTH", "AVG--ALL STOCKS"
95     REM
97     PRINT
100    REM -- NOW FIND MONTHLY AVERAGES
105    FOR J = 1 TO M
107      LET T1 = 0
110      FOR I = 1 TO N
112        LET T1 = T1 + S(I,J)
115      NEXT I
118      PRINT J, T1/N
120    NEXT J
125    REM
130    STOP
140    END
```

Notice the way in which the loops are nested. In lines 50 through 80 the object is to compute the average price and standard deviation of price for each stock; thus the outside loop changes the value of I, which is used to indicate the row number. But in lines 105 through 120 the object is to compute the average price for each month; thus the outside loop changes the value of J, which is used to indicate the column number.

Reserving Space

In standard systems, unless you explicitly reserve a specific amount of space, the computer will reserve enough for you to use subscripts as high as 10 for both lists and tables. Hence, references to P(10) and S(10,10) are perfectly legal even if you have not previously reserved space for list P and table S.

But you may want the computer to provide more or less space than this (more when you need more; less when you need less and the space is required for other lists and/or tables). To do this you indicate the desired dimensions explicitly in a DIM (for dimension) statement:

```
  10    DIM A(250)
 500    DIM B(3)
3150    DIM X(8,15)
```

The first statement reserves space for 250 items in list A. The second statement reserves space for three items in list B. The third statement reserves space for eight rows and fifteen columns in table X.[4] You may reserve space for more than one list and/or table with a single DIM statement; the entries are simply separated by commas:

$$5 \quad DIM \ A(250), \ B(3), \ X(8,15)$$

If a list or table is to be dimensioned, the applicable DIM statement should precede any other reference to it in the program.

One other thing: Remember, the space to be reserved must be indicated *explicitly* — no expressions allowed in a DIM statement.

A Small Restriction

Generally you may use a subscripted variable (list or table reference) anywhere you are allowed to use a simple (unsubscripted) variable. There is one exception, however. The variable altered during execution of a FOR-NEXT loop should be an unsubscripted variable. This limitation refers only to the variable mentioned immediately after FOR in the FOR statement (and again after NEXT in the NEXT statement). The initial, terminal, and step values may involve any expression at all, including subscripted variables.

Problems

1. Table Z has ten rows and ten columns. Write a set of statements to set all the entries to zero.
2. What output will be produced by the following program?

---

4. As stated earlier, standard systems also reserve space for a zero'th item in lists and a zero'th row and column in tables.

```
10    FOR I = 1 TO 8
11       LET B(I) = 2 *I
12    NEXT I
20    FOR J = 1 TO 6
21       PRINT B(J),
22    NEXT J
30    STOP
```

3. What output will be produced by the following program?

```
10    FOR K = 1 TO 4
11       LET Q(K,K) = 9
12    NEXT K
20    FOR K = 1 TO 4
21       FOR L = K+1 TO 4
22          LET Q(K,L) = 1
23       NEXT L
24    NEXT K
30    FOR K = 1 TO 4
31       FOR L = 1 TO K-1
32          LET Q(K,L) = 0
33       NEXT L
34    NEXT K
40    FOR K = 1 TO 4
41       FOR L = 1 TO 4
42          PRINT Q(K,L),
43       NEXT L
44       PRINT
45    NEXT K
50    STOP
```

4. Assume you have been given a program which reads in list X and sorts the numbers into ascending order. X has 50 items and has been previously dimensioned. Write a program segment (to add to the given program) which "moves" the items in X to another list Y, so that Y is sorted in *descending* order. When you are finished, you should still have list X in its original order. (Don't forget to dimension Y.)

5. Assume that you have been asked to expand the program given in this chapter for setting up the table of distances for direct routes between pairs of cities. Add the necessary instructions to find and print the shortest distance from city 1 to each of the other cities. Hints:

    (a) Let S(J) be the shortest distance from city 1 to city J.
    (b) To get started, let S(J) = D(1,J).
    (c) Now, assume that S(3) is the current shortest distance from city 1 to city 3, and that S(3) + D(3,5) is less than the current value of S(5); what would you do?
    (d) In general, assume that S(I) + D(I,J) is less than S(J); what would you do?

Remark: This is a difficult problem. If you conquer it, you are well on your way to programming rather complicated procedures; however, even if you fail, the situation is far from hopeless.

Answers

1.

```
10    FOR I = 1 TO 10
11      FOR J = 1 TO 10
12        LET Z(I,J) = 0
13      NEXT J
14    NEXT I
```

It is good practice to "clear" lists and tables before starting processing. In some cases it is absolutely essential.

2.

```
2     4     6     8     10
12
```

Remember that there is no B(I) or B(J); only B(1), B(2), and so on.

3.

```
9     1     1     1
0     9     1     1
0     0     9     1
0     0     0     9
```

If you didn't get this right, get out a piece of paper and play computer, doing exactly what the instructions tell you to do.

4. Would you believe?

```
1000    DIM Y(50)
1001    FOR I = 1 TO 50
1002      LET Y(51-I) = X(I)
1003    NEXT I
```

If you don't believe it, make up some phony numbers, stick them in list X, and then see what the program does to them. This is, of course, just one of several ways (but a very efficient one, at that) to solve the problem.

5. The program statements through and including line 50 are the same as those shown in the earlier example. A possible set of additional statements

to solve the problem follows:

```
51    REM -- SET UP INITIAL VALUES
52    FOR J = 2 TO 10
53      LET S(J) = D(I,J)
54    NEXT J
55    REM
60    REM -- CHECK EACH VALUE FOR POSSIBLE IMPROVEMENT
61    LET Z = 0
62    FOR J = 2 TO 10
63      FOR I = 2 TO 10
64        IF I = J THEN 69
65        IF (S(I) + D(I,J)) >= S(J) THEN 69
66        REM -- SHORTER ROUTE FOUND
67        LET Z = 1
68        LET S(J) = S(I) + D(I,J)
69      NEXT I
70    NEXT J
71    IF Z = 1 THEN 60
75    REM
80    REM -- PRINT RESULTS
82    FOR J = 2 TO 10
83      IF S(J) = 9999 THEN 86
84      PRINT "SHORTEST DISTANCE TO",J,"FROM 1 =";S(J)
85      GO TO 87
86      PRINT "CITY"; J; "CANNOT BE REACHED FROM CITY 1"
87    NEXT J
90    STOP
```

see how the program works, use the following data:

```
901   DATA 1, 2, 10
902   DATA 1, 4, 50
903   DATA 2, 3, 90
904   DATA 2, 4, 30
905   DATA 3, 4, 40
906   DATA -1, -1, -1
```

CHAPTER 8

Functions and Subroutines

Functions

Periodically, you may want to calculate some type of *function*. For example, you may want to find the logarithm of a number. Several of the more useful functions of this type can be obtained by simply asking for them. The function desired is usually indicated by a three-letter name. The value to be used is usually indicated explicitly or implicitly in parentheses following the function name. Thus LOG(8) refers to the natural logarithm of eight, and LOG(A + B) to the natural logarithm of the number found by adding A to B. The expression in the parentheses is called the *argument* of the function; it is evaluated and the resulting number used as indicated.

A function may be used in any expression. For example:

```
10    LET Z = A + LOG(3)
20    LET Q3 = A + (5*LOG(3))
30    IF B + LOG(C) > 50 THEN 433
40    PRINT LOG(C) / LOG(B+8)
```

When the computer encounters a function, it:

1. Evaluates the expression in the parentheses.
2. Applies the rules specified for the function in question (e.g., takes the logarithm of the number).

3. Uses the resulting number as if it had appeared instead of the function name and its argument.

Ten functions available for the asking are described below. For convenience, each is written here with an argument of X, but of course the argument may be any legal expression.

Function	Gives
LOG(X)	The natural logarithm of X
EXP(X)	The value obtained by raising e ($= 2.71828...$) to the X'th power
ABS(X)	The absolute value of X
SQR(X)	The square root of X
INT(X)	The largest integer not greater than X. For example: if X is 9.8, INT(X) = 9
SIN(X)	The sine of X; X must be expressed in radians
COS(X)	The cosine of X; X must be expressed in radians
TAN(X)	The tangent of X; X must be expressed in radians
ATN(X)	The arctangent of X; the arctangent is given in radians
SGN(X)	IF X > 0, SGN(X) = 1
	If X = 0, SGN(X) = 0
	If X<0, SGN(X) = − 1

Random Numbers

A computer may be used to simulate events that happen in a somewhat random manner. One way to do this would involve reading in as data a list of random numbers. However, this is not necessary, for the computer acts as if it has its own list already (actually it computes numbers as required, but you need not concern yourself with such details). Each number in the list lies between zero and 1. If you were to produce a great many numbers, you would find that they fall rather uniformly over the range (in other words, they come from a uniformly distributed population of random numbers between zero and 1). You can get the next number from the list by simply writing:[1]

RND

This can appear in any expression; in form it is like the regular functions, although its value is obtained in a very different manner. When the computer encounters RND, it simply substitutes the next number from its list of random numbers and proceeds.

For example, the following program:

---

1. Nonstandard systems may require a "dummy argument" that is not used, e.g., RND(1).

```
10     FOR I = 1 TO 5
11        LET Z = RND
12        PRINT Z
13     NEXT I
14     STOP
```

might generate the following output:

```
.151432
.901628
.012963
.594318
.770312
```

To simulate the results obtained by flipping a coin five times, simply write the following:

```
20     FOR I = 1 TO 5
21        IF RND <= .5 THEN 24
22        PRINT "HEADS"
23        GO TO 25
24        PRINT "TAILS"
25     NEXT I
26     STOP
```

Each time statement 21 is executed, a random number (the next one in the list) will be obtained; if it is greater than .5, the computer will print HEADS; if it is not, the computer will print TAILS.

Would you like a random number between 0 and 38? Simply write this:

$$10 \quad \text{LET R} = 38 * \text{RND}$$

Obviously, 38 times a number falling between 0 and 1 must give a number between 0 and 38. If you would like R to be an integer between 1 and 38, simply write this:[2]

$$10 \quad \text{LET R} = \text{INT}(1 + (38 * \text{RND}))$$

One problem may bother you. The first time RND is encountered, the first number in the computer's random number list is substituted; the second time, the second number is substituted, and so forth. If you want to start at a different place in the list each time you run your program, you could tell the com-

---

2. In the unlikely event that the random number turns out to be exactly 1.0, this statement would set R to 39. To insure against this, you could follow line 10 with

$$11 \quad \text{IF R} = 39 \text{ THEN } 10$$

puter to look at some of the initial entries. Then it would begin the real work with numbers lying farther down in the list. For example, you might preface the actual computations with:

```
10    READ N
11    FOR I = 1 TO N
12       LET X = RND
13    NEXT I
```

and then put some arbitrary value for N in a data statement.

Standard systems allow you to generate random numbers beginning at an unpredictable starting point in the list. The command:

RANDOMIZE

tells the computer to pick a new starting point in a more or less random fashion (the current time on an internal clock is generally used for this purpose).[3]

Subroutines

By now you have undoubtedly had the following experience: You have a procedure requiring several statements; moreover, the procedure needs to be followed in several places in your program. It is obviously a bother to rewrite all the statements repeatedly in every part of the program in which the procedure must be followed. You need some way to write the statements once and then refer to them as required. To do this you write the procedure as a subroutine. Whenever you want to execute it, you tell the computer to go to the beginning of the subroutine but to remember where it was before beginning the subroutine. When the statements have been executed, the computer is expected to return to the appropriate place in the program.

The two new statements required for subroutines are GOSUB and RETURN. GOSUB is similar to a GO TO: the difference is that when the computer is told to GO TO 200, it goes to line 200 and promptly forgets where it was when it transferred there. But when it is told to GOSUB 200, it transfers to line number 200 and remembers where it was prior to the transfer. Later, when the computer encounters a RETURN statement, it will automatically go to the statement following the GOSUB from which it transferred.[4]

---

3. Nonstandard systems accomplish this in different ways (for example, via the appearance of RND(0) in a program). Some systems allow the user to control the starting point via a "seed" value. For example, the appearance of RND(-8) in a program might start a new sequence of random numbers using 8 as a seed.

4. If desired, a space may be left between GO and SUB.

To illustrate the use of subroutines, assume that the following statements occur somewhere in a program:

```
200    LET F = N
201    FOR M = N-1 TO 1 STEP -1
202       LET F = F * M
203    NEXT M
204    RETURN
```

This is the routine to compute the factorial of a number. Now assume that you want the factorial of some number, for example, X3. You simply put its value in box N and call in the subroutine:

```
10    LET N = X3
11    GOSUB 200
12    PRINT F
```

When the computer reaches statement 11, it transfers to statement 200, making a note of the fact that it got there from statement 11. Statement 200 is then executed, and the factorial is computed by the statements following it. Eventually, statement 204 is reached. The computer then returns to the statement following number 11 — statement 12.

Perhaps you need to calculate the factoral of X8 at some later point in your program. Just say:

```
56    LET N = X8
57    GOSUB 200
58    PRINT F
```

This example illustrates another advantage of the subroutine. Once you have written a set of statements to compute a factorial and checked them out to insure that they work, you can regard them as a "black box." Any time you need a factorial, just write GOSUB 200. This is extremely helpful when you are writing large programs. You simply break the program into modules that are logically distinct, programming each as a subroutine. In fact, it is not unusual to encounter programs that look like this:

```
10    REM --- READ DATA
11       GOSUB 100
12    REM -- PROCESS DATA
13       GOSUB 200
14    REM -- PRINT DATA
15       GOSUB 300
16    REM -- RETURN TO PROCESS ANOTHER SET OF DATA
17       GO TO 10
```

The statements required to perform the desired operations would then follow. Although the first statement in a subroutine can be of any type, it is good practice to let it be a remark indicating the purpose of the subroutine:

100   REM — SUBROUTINE TO READ DATA

There are many advantages to be gained if programs are written in this modular manner. It is even possible to have different people program different parts of a problem. Of course, there must be close coordination so that the same variable will not be used inadvertently for different purposes in different subroutines.

You may have GOSUB statements within subroutines. For example, consider the following (nonsense) program:

```
10      READ N
11      GOSUB 100
12      PRINT Q, R, Z
13      STOP
20      REM
100     REM -- SUBROUTINE A
101     LET Q = 2 * N
102     GOSUB 200
103     LET R = Q / Z
104     RETURN
105     REM
200     REM -- SUBROUTINE B
201     LET Z = 8
202     FOR I = 1 TO N
203        LET Z = I * Z
204     NEXT I
205     RETURN
```

When statement 11 is reached, the computer transfers to statement 100. It soon reaches statement 102, which sends it to statement 200. Eventually, a RETURN is encountered at statement 205, and the computer returns to the place from which it departed most recently (in this case, statement 103). Later, upon encountering another RETURN it goes to statement 12, as intended.

It is perfectly acceptable for a GOSUB statement to appear inside a FOR-NEXT loop, even if the subroutine itself is not inside the loop.

However, there are some things to watch out for when using subroutines. Never allow the computer to "fall" into a subroutine without going there via a GOSUB, as in:

```
10      REM -- MAIN PROGRAM
20      READ P
25      IF P > 0 THEN 40
30      GOSUB 100
```

```
   40    PRINT P
   45    REM
  100    REM -- SUBROUTINE
  110    LET P = INT(ABS(P))
  120    RETURN
```

Why not? Because when the computer comes to the RETURN, it won't know to which statement it should return. GOSUB is the only statement that provides it with a memory of where it has been.

Unless you know exactly what you are doing, never allow a subroutine to contain a GOSUB to itself. This is called *recursion*, and experienced programmers sometimes use it for special kinds of problems. But if "self-calling" subroutines are used inadvertently or without a thorough understanding of recursion, the computer may find itself in an "infinite loop" (i.e., circling through your program forever).

User-defined Functions

The most important thing to remember about functions is that each represents the value obtained by executing a specific computation. Instead of writing out the computation every time you wish to use it, you simply refer to the appropriate function by name and let BASIC substitute the resulting value for you. For example, LOG(X) represents "the value obtained by computing the natural logarithm of the expression X, whatever the latter might be." As the value of X changes, so does LOG(X). And TAN(X) is the name given to "the value obtained by computing the tangent of expression X."

So far, all the functions discussed have had something else in common: They are supplied as part of BASIC. You might call them "canned" functions. Actually, there is no reason to limit yourself to canned functions; you can define your own. Such functions are called *user-defined functions* (naturally), but in other respects they are like ordinary functions: Each must yield a single value.

The DEF Statement

Suppose you wish to compute the volume of a sphere, given by:

$$V = \frac{4}{3} \pi R^3$$

for various values of R. You could write the formula in a subroutine:

```
101    REM -- COMPUTE VOLUME OF A SPHERE
101    LET V = (4/3)*3.1416*(R^3)
102    RETURN
```

Then, if you need the results for two values of R, you could say:

```
50    LET R = 4.5
52    GOSUB 100
54    PRINT "VOLUME OF A SPHERE OF RADIUS "; R; "IS "; V
56    LET R = 27.8
58    GOSUB 100
60    PRINT "VOLUME OF A SPHERE OF RADIUS "; R; "IS "; V
```

But why bother? Since you really want to compute a single value (i.e., volume), why not simply define the formula as a function? You can, by using the DEF statement. First, think of a name for the function. The name must be three letters, the first two of which are FN. Obviously, this restricts you to a choice of one of twenty-six names. Suppose you select FNV. Then you might define the function like this:

$$10 \quad \text{DEF FNV} = (4/3) * (3.1416) * (R \wedge 3)$$

Later, you can simplify your program:

```
50    LET R = 4.5
52    PRINT "VOLUME OF A SPHERE OF RADIUS "; R; "IS "; FNV
54    LET R = 27.8
56    PRINT "VOLUME OF A SPHERE OF RADIUS "; R; "IS "; FNV
```

Whenever the computer sees the two letters FN followed by another letter, it looks for a DEF statement for that function. When it finds the right one, the function is evaluated (like any other expression), and the value is substituted for the function name in the statement in which it was used.

Notice that FNV has no arguments. The computer merely has to look up the current value of R, plug it into the formula, evaluate the latter, and return the value.

You can define other functions, too. Just include a DEF statement for each one. Like canned functions, each may be included wherever an arithmetic expression is legal. Here are some examples:

```
790    LET H2 = LOG(ABS(FNR + FNS)) + (A * B5 * FNN)
792    PRINT FNW ^ 2; SQR(FNQ)
793    IF FNA <= (47 * FNB) THEN 800
```

Several other points should be made. First, the DEF statement should appear before you actually refer to a function. Second, the DEF statement is never executed directly; it serves to provide the appropriate formula whenever you refer to the function in *another* statement. Thus it is perfectly acceptable to intermix DEF's with other program statements, as in this program:

```
100    REM -- METRIC CONVERSION PROGRAM
101    REM -- READ IN CENTIMETERS
104    READ C
105    REM -- CONVERSION FUNCTIONS
106    DEF FNI = C * 0.393700
107    DEF FNF = FNI * 0.083333
110    REM -- CONVERT CENTIMETERS TO INCHES, FEET, AND YARDS
112    PRINT "CENTIMETERS "; C; "INCHES "; FNI;
113    PRINT "FEET "; FNF; "YARDS "; FNF/3
120    GO TO 101
```

Third, notice another thing about this program—FNF is defined in terms of FNI. No problem. When the computer attempts to compute the value of FNF, it will see that it must compute FNI first and use the resulting value to determine FNF. If you can keep things straight, so can the computer. Just don't let your definitions get circular. Here is an example of what not to do:

```
10    DEF FNZ = (FNY*100) + X^2
20    DEF FNY = EXP(W)/LOG(FNZ)
```

Although it is completely legal to use any proper expression in a function definition (including other functions), you should never define any two so that they refer to one another.

Functions with Arguments

DEF statements may also be used to define functions with arguments. For example, the volume function could be defined as follows:

$$10 \quad \text{DEF FNV}(X) = (4/3) * 3.1416 * (X \wedge 3)$$

FNV now has a single argument. But why X instead of R? Merely to point out the difference between a *parameter* and any other program variable. Anything appearing as an argument in a function definition is a parameter, which must be a simple (i.e., unsubscripted) numeric variable. Hence, X is a parameter of FNV. Suppose elsewhere in your program you said:

$$50 \quad \text{LET V2} = \text{FNV}(R)/2$$

When the computer encounters line 50, it will substitute the current value of

R for X wherever X appears in the formula for FNV, compute the function's value, and plug that value into the formula in line 50. A parameter, like X in this case, serves to hold the place of the value you will later specify. You could also say:

$$73 \quad \text{LET W(I)} = \text{FNV}(3.5) + (A1 * W7)$$

or:

$$159 \quad \text{LET H6} = (\text{FNV}(2 * H7)/(2/3)) + \text{EXP(Y)}$$

In the first case, the number 3.5 would be substituted for X; in the second, the value 2 * H7 would be substituted. Whenever you refer to a function in another statement, you may substitute *any* legal expression for the function parameter appearing in the DEF statement.

Parameters have another important characteristic, which is illustrated by this (nonsense) program:

```
  5   REM -- FUNCTION DEFINITIONS
 10   DEF FNN(Y) = (1/SQR(P))*EXP((-(.5))*(Y^2))
 20   DEF FNM(Y) = A*((1 - (Y^N))/(1 - Y))
100   REM -- INITIALIZE VARIABLES
101   LET P = 3.1416
102   READ A, N, X
103   REM -- USE FUNCTIONS
104   LET Y = (1/COS(X))*FNM(3.7)
105   LET Z = FNN(0.24) - FNN(0.23)
106   LET W = FNM(Z)
107   PRINT Y; Z; W; FNM(X)
```

Notice that the DEF statements for both FNN(Y) and FNM(Y) specify a single *parameter* (Y). Notice, too, that *variable* Y has been used in lines 104 and 107. Does this mean the computer must use the value of variable Y when evaluating FNN(Y) and FNM(Y)? No. The name given to a function parameter is strictly arbitrary. Since the computer doesn't know in advance what number you will want substituted for the parameter when you refer to a function, you may choose any unsubscripted variable name for it. The name you choose has meaning *only* within the function definition (even though it may be the same as the name of a variable used outside the DEF statement).

How does the computer know when you are referring to *variable* Y and not *parameter* Y (or vice-versa)? It's really not so difficult. Look at line 105 of the program. It says: "Compute the value of FNN(Y), replacing parameter Y in the function definition by 0.24. Then compute the value of FNN(Y), replacing parameter Y by 0.23. Subtract the second result from the first, and store the difference in Z." *Only* if line 105 had said something like this:

$$105 \quad \text{LET Z} = \text{FNN(Y)}$$

would the value of *variable* Y have been used to evaluate the function. Of course, when not evaluating a function with parameter Y, the computer assumes that all references to Y are references to *variable* Y.

Another way to approach the matter is to think of a DEF statement as a tiny program within a larger one. The function may define a special "parameter-mailbox" that only that function can use. Thus, we often call parameters *local variables* because they refer to mailboxes "owned" by DEF statements and not available to the rest of the program. Of course, any variable mentioned in a DEF statement that is not a parameter refers to a mailbox in the larger program. (In line 10, for example, the computer has to go outside the function definition to obtain the value for P.) We often call these variables *global variables*. The distinction is sufficiently important that you should understand it thoroughly.

Playing Roulette

Many of the points in this chapter are illustrated in the following program. We assume that a prospective gambler wishes to try certain strategies for playing roulette in a simulated casino. His betting strategy is called a *martingale*. He begins with a basic bet (B); whenever he wins, he returns to his basic bet. Whenever he loses, however, his next bet is double the previous (lost) amount — unless his money is insufficient, in which case he bets everything he has. The player continues until he either exhausts his capital or reaches some predetermined upper limit (U).

Our gambler is convinced that his martingale strategy is sound, but he is uncertain as to whether he ought to put his money on number 1 each time or on "red" (there are fifteen red numbers). If he chooses the former, he wins thirty-five times his bet if successful. If he chooses the latter, his successes will be more frequent, but he will win only an amount equal to his bet each time. The gambler wants to be able to indicate in his data which of the two playing strategies is to be simulated. He also wants to be able to indicate whether or not a complete record of results (spin by spin) should be printed.

The program is relatively straightforward. The roulette wheel is assumed to have thirty-eight numbers and to be fair. Notice the extensive use of subroutines. This makes it easy to make changes in the program; for example, to alter strategies, calculate the effects of unbalanced wheels and the like. Note also the use of P and S9 as "switches" to select the appropriate subroutines to be employed. Such techniques are essential for the professional programmer, and they can be valuable for you as well. The program (printed with indentations for clarity) follows:

```
10    REM -- PROGRAM TO SIMULATE ROULETTE PLAY
11    REM -- READ DATA
12       GOSUB 100
13    REM -- PERFORM INITIAL PROCESSING
14       GOSUB 200
15    REM -- SPIN WHEEL
16       GOSUB 250
17    REM -- FIND RESULTS (DEPENDING ON STRATEGY)
18    IF S9 = 1 THEN 21
19       GOSUB 300
20          GO TO 22
21       GOSUB 350
22    REM -- PRINT RESULTS IF DESIRED
23    IF P = 0 THEN 25
24       GOSUB 400
25    REM -- TEST FOR COMPLETION AND SELECT NEXT BET
26       GOSUB 500
27    REM -- SPIN AGAIN
28       GO TO 15
30    REM
100   REM -- SUBROUTINE TO READ DATA
101   READ C, B, U, N, P, S9
102   PRINT "TOTAL CAPITAL =", C
103   PRINT "BASIC BET =", B
104   PRINT "UPPER LIMIT =", U
105   PRINT "INITIAL SPINS =", N
106   IF P = 0 THEN 109
107      PRINT "COMPLETE RECORD REQUESTED"
108         GO TO 110
109      PRINT "ONLY FINAL RESULTS REQUESTED "
110   IF S9 = 1 THEN 113
111      PRINT "STRATEGY IS TO BET ON RED EACH TIME"
112         GO TO 114
113      PRINT "STRAGETY IS TO BET ON 1 EACH TIME"
114      PRINT
115   RETURN
117   REM
200   REM -- SUBROUTINE TO PERFORM INITIAL PROCESSING
201   REM -- MAKE INITIAL SPINS
202   FOR I = 1 TO N
203      LET Z = RND
204   NEXT I
205   REM -- SET UP INITIAL WAGER
206   LET W = B
207   REM -- SET NUMBER OF SPINS TO ZERO
208   LET S = 0
209   RETURN
210   REM
250   REM -- SUBROUTINE TO SPIN WHEEL
251   DEF FNX(R) = INT(1+38*R)
252   LET R = RND
253   IF FNX(R) = 39 THEN 252
254   LET S = S + 1
255   RETURN
256   REM
300   REM -- SUBROUTINE FOR STRATEGY 0
301   IF FNX(R) <= 15 THEN 306
302   REM -- LOST
303      LET O9 = 0
304      LET C = C - W
305      RETURN
306   REM -- WON
307      LET O9 = 1
308      LET C = C + W
309      RETURN
310   REM
350   REM -- SUBROUTINE FOR STRATEGY 1
351   IF FNX(R) = 1 THEN 356
352   REM -- LOST
```

```
353      LET 09 = 0
354      LET C = C - W
355      RETURN
356   REM -- WON
357      LET 09 = 1
358      LET C = C + (35*W)
359      RETURN
360   REM
400   REM -- SUBROUTINE TO PRINT RESULTS OF A SPIN
401   PRINT "SPIN NUMBER", S
402   PRINT "YOU BET", W
403   PRINT "WHEEL CAME UP", R
404   PRINT "YOU NOW HAVE", C
405   PRINT
406   RETURN
407   REM
500   REM -- TEST FOR COMPLETION AND SELECT NEXT BET
501   IF C = 0 THEN 520
502   IF C >= U THEN 530
503   REM -- PLAY AGAIN
504   IF 09 = 0 THEN 510
505   REM -- PREVIOUS BET WON
506      LET W = B
507      GO TO 515
510   REM -- PREVIOUS BET LOST, DOUBLE IT
511      LET W = 2 * W
515   REM -- CHECK CAPITAL
516   IF C > W THEN 519
517   REM -- LOWER WAGER
518      LET W = C
519   RETURN
520   REM -- WIPED OUT
521      PRINT "SORRY -- WIPED OUT AFTER ";S;"SPINS"
522      STOP
530   REM -- MADE IT
531     PRINT "UPPER LIMIT REACHED AFTER";S;"SPINS"
532     PRINT "YOUR CAPITAL IS NOW", C
533     PRINT "CONGRATULATIONS"
534   STOP
999   END
```

Canned Programs

Many people who use computers do not attempt to master a programming
language at all; instead, they simply rely on professional programmers who
have (it is hoped) anticipated their needs when preparing programs. Certainly
one need not program his or her own routine to do regression analysis, or linear programming, or any of a number of generally utilized techniques. It is
far more efficient for a professional programmer to devote time to preparing a
general purpose, well written, and highly efficient program for such an application. Such "production," "canned," or "package" programs should meet the
following criteria:

1. They should be extremely simple to use: this means that input can be
   prepared by simply following a few straightforward instructions.
2. They should be truly general purpose; several variations of the

technique should be available with only a few alterations in input data required to obtain a different variation (unfortunately, this criterion is often in conflict with the first).

3. They should provide output describing the results explicitly and requiring little or no knowledge of the underlying (solution) technique on the part of the user.

4. They should anticipate virtually any type of error that the user might make when preparing his input data; moreover, such errors should be identified on the output when detected.

5. Finally, they should be efficient (require minimal computer time) and thoroughly checked (they should work).

The language in which a program is written is of little concern to the user who wants to do exactly what the program is designed to do. But it is not unusual to find that a few changes in the program will be required if it is to serve the exact purpose the user had in mind. Under these conditions the language used is important, as is the program's documentation. Since no program can be truly general purpose, some canned programs are written as subroutines (or sets of subroutines); the user is then expected to incorporate them in a program written to serve his particular needs.

Problems

1. Write a statement to round variable Z to the nearest integer (whole number); assume that Z is positive.

2. Write a statement to round variable Z to the nearest tenth (i.e., one decimal place); assume that Z is positive.

3. Assume that variable G represents gross pay in dollars. Write a statement to round it to the nearest cent.

4. Write a subroutine that will round variable A to the nearest value with N places to the right of the decimal point.

5. Write some statements to set up a list Z containing the logarithms of the first N numbers in some other list X.

6. What is the output from the following program segment?

```
  5    LET X = 0
 10    GOSUB 100
 20    PRINT 4
 30    STOP
100    PRINT 1,
110    IF X = 0 THEN 200
115    RETURN
200    PRINT 2,
202    LET X = 1
205    GOSUB 100
210    PRINT 3,
212    RETURN
```

Note in this case we have a subroutine calling itself. Will it get into an "infinite loop"? Why, or why not?

7. Write a program segment that will generate fifty random integers between (and including) the values of 1 and 3. Print each as "one," "two," or "three."

8. Write a statement that assigns the following value to B7: The logarithm of the absolute value of the sine of the square root of the integer portion of Z9.

9. Write a function that finds the common logarithm (log to the base 10) of any positive number. The formula is:

$$LOG_{10}(X) = LOG_e(X)\, LOG_{10}(e)$$

$LOG_{10}(e)$ is a constant; it equals approximately 0.4343.

Answers

1.
$$10 \quad LET\ Z = INT(Z + .5)$$

2.
$$10 \quad LET\ Z = .1 * INT((10 * Z) + .5)$$

3.
$$10 \quad LET\ G = .01 * INT((100 * G) + .5)$$

4.

```
100   LET P=10^N
101   LET A=(1/P)*INT((P*A)+.5)
102   RETURN
```

5.

```
100   FOR I = I TO N
101      LET Z(I) = LOG(X(I))
102   NEXT I
```

6.
$$1 \quad 2 \quad 1 \quad 3 \quad 4$$

The computer will not get into an unending loop because the value of X is altered after the first pass through the subroutine. On the second pass through, it is tested to see if the value has been changed. Upon finding out it has been, the computer promptly returns to the place from which it came via the GOSUB.

7. One solution is:

```
10    FOR L = 1 TO 50
12       LET R = INT(1 + RND(0)*3)
14       IF R = 4 THEN 12
16       IF R > 1 THEN 22
18       PRINT "ONE"
20       GO TO 35
22       IF R > 2 THEN 28
24       PRINT "TWO"
26       GO TO 35
28       PRINT "THREE"
35    NEXT L
```

8.

$$\text{LET } B7 = \text{LOG(ABS(SIN(SQR(INT(Z9)))))}$$

9. This will do it:

$$\text{DEF FNL(X)} = \text{LOG(X)} * (0.4343)$$

PART II

Extended BASIC

CHAPTER 9

More on Strings

Chapter 5 showed some of the uses of string variables in BASIC programs. Recall that a string variable is essentially a mailbox that may contain a sequence of alphabetic and/or numeric characters. As we noted, string variables may be used in LET, PRINT, READ, INPUT, and IF statements. The present chapter suggests some additional ways that strings can be used in these statements.

String Lists

Strings may be put into lists and tables just as numeric values may be. Legal string list (or table) names are the same as for simple string variables: A$, B$, . . . , and so on, through Z$. If you want to read ten strings into list R$, you can do so by saying:

```
10    FOR I = 1 TO 10
20       READ R$(I)
30    NEXT I
```

After execution of this program, each element in R$ will contain a single string. The INPUT command may also be used to "fill" string lists; hence, by replacing line 20 of the above program with the statement

20   INPUT R$(I)

the program would instead obtain ten strings from the terminal and place them in list R$.

As before, if you anticipate putting more than ten items into a list, you must reserve space in a DIM statement. Numeric lists and tables may be included in the same DIM statement. It is legal to say:

DIM T$(20), P(30,10), W(11), S$(22,5)

On most systems, the dimension of a string list or table specifies the number of strings and not the number of characters in any one string; thus, the dimension of S$ above indicates that there are 22 rows, each containing a string of (normally) up to 18 characters, and 5 columns, each containing a string.[1]

Sorting and Comparing Strings

As we noted in chapter 5, strings may be compared using IF statements. This is a very useful capability, for it allows (among other things) the alphabetization of lists of names, places, or other information. To show how we might perform such a task, it is first necessary to explain the rules the computer follows in deciding when one string is "greater than" or "less than" another.

Consider the comparison:

If   A$ <> B$ THEN 10

To determine whether or not to proceed to line 10, the computer embarks on the following procedure: It compares the first character of the string in A$ with the first character of the string in B$. If the two characters are the same, it compares the second characters of both, then the third, and so on. When it finds a character in A$ that is not equal to the corresponding one in B$, that character becomes the basis for the decision. If it is of lower rank than its counterpart in B$, then A$ is "less than" B$, and the computer would go to line 10. If it is of higher rank, the first string is the "greater" of the two, and again the computer would go to line 10. And if the computer runs out of characters in one of the strings before finding any mismatches, the shorter string is considered the "lesser." Only if both strings are exactly the same, including having the same length, will the computer consider them to be equal.

The procedure is just like the one lexicographers use to order the words in a dictionary. Hence, we can think of strings as having some sort of lexicographic ordering that IF statements can interrogate for us. We might want to know if "1A" comes before (i.e., is less than) "2A" in the computer's "dictionary," for

1. The maximum number of characters that can be placed in a single string variable or element in a string list (table) varies from 1 to 255 or more, depending on the computer system.

example. Or, whether the string "X7" comes after (i.e., is greater than) "X65."

Obviously, in order to know how the computer orders strings in its dictionary, it is necessary to know how it ranks individual characters. Two ranking rules are:

1. Letters (A to Z) are ranked in alphabetic order, from lowest (A) to highest (Z).
2. Digits (0 to 9) are ranked in numeric order, from lowest (0) to highest (9).

This is just what you'd want it to do. "JOHNSON" comes before "JONES"; "1A" comes before "2A"; "676" comes before "677", "X7" comes after "X65", and so on. And because ties are broken on the basis of length, "SAM" comes before "SAMUEL" and "15" comes before "150".

Comparisons between a letter and a digit, a digit and a special symbol (such as *,/,$,%), or a special symbol and a letter should be undertaken with great care. In many systems all letters are ranked higher than digits; in others, the reverse may be true. Thus one system may rank "B5" greater than "5B"; another may not. Moral: Avoid making such comparisons unless you know your computer's ranking rules.

It is important to remember that although strings may contain digits, they have no numeric value. Even though the string "123" may be "less than" the string "1234", comparisons between a string and a numeric constant are meaningless (as well as illegal). Strings can be compared only with other strings, and numbers compared only with other numbers.

String comparisons can be used in conjunction with string lists to sort information into a desired sequence, such as into alphabetic order. Suppose, for instance, that we have read a list of 100 names into two lists using the following statements:

```
10    DIM W$(100), F$(100)
20    FOR I = 1 TO 100
30      READ W$(I), F$(I)
40    NEXT I
```

The data look like this:

```
900    DATA "MARKOWITZ", "HARRY"
910    DATA "RUBINSTEIN", "MARK"
920    DATA "ALBERTS", "WILLIAM"
930    DATA "PAGE", "ALFRED"
940    DATA "DILLON", "VICTORIA"
```

Thus, each person's last name has been read into list W$ and his or her first name into the corresponding position in list F$.

Now, suppose we wish to rearrange lists W$ and F$ in ascending order alphabetically by last name and for identical last names, alphabetically by first name. When we have finished, the last name closest to the beginning of the alphabet will appear in W$(1) with its associated first name in F$(1); the next closest last name in W$(2) with its associated first name in F$(2), and so forth.

Fortunately, we can accomplish this task by making only minor revisions to the sort routine introduced in chapter 7. Here is a revision that works:

```
50    REM -- SORT FIRST AND LAST NAMES
60       LET S = 0
70    FOR I = 1 TO 99
80       IF W$(I) = W$(I+1) THEN 180
90       IF W$(I) < W$(I+1) THEN 230
100      LET S = S + 1
110      LET Z$ = W$(I)
120      LET X$ = F$(I)
130      LET W$(I) = W$(I+1)
140      LET F$(I) = F$(I+1)
150      LET W$(I+1) = Z$
160      LET F$(I+1) = X$
170      GO TO 230
180      IF F$(I) <= F$(I+1) THEN 230
190      LET S = S + 1
200      LET X$ = F$(I)
210      LET F$(I) = F$(I+1)
220      LET F$(I+1) = X$
230   NEXT I
240      IF S > 0 THEN 60
250   REM -- SORT IS COMPLETED
```

Notice that if the routine comes across two last names that are identical, it checks the first names to see if they are out of alphabetic sequence. If they are—as would be the case if SMITH, TOM preceded SMITH, HARRIET—only the first names need be rearranged (i.e., the names in list F$) in order to achieve the proper ordering. Notice also that, since blanks are important in strings, each first and last name should be free of blanks appearing anywhere. (See exercise 2 at the end of this chapter.)

The CHANGE Statement

Some systems have special features that allow you to take strings apart and create new ones, look for the occurrence of particular characters in a string, or find the length of a string.

One such feature is the CHANGE statement. It changes a string variable into a numeric list by substituting "code numbers" for each of the characters in the string. Suppose, for example, that V$ = "HELLO". Then the instruction:

CHANGE V$ TO V

causes a list V to be created whose elements are code numbers representing the letters H, E, L, L, O. The zero'th item in V will contain a number equal to the number of characters in V$.[2] Assume the codes for the letters in V$ are those given below:

Letter	Code
E	69
L	76
H	72
O	79

After the CHANGE statement has been executed, list V will look like this:

$$V(0) = 5$$
$$V(1) = 72$$
$$V(2) = 69$$
$$V(3) = 76$$
$$V(4) = 76$$
$$V(5) = 79$$

The code for the first character of V$ is in $V(1)$, the code for the second character is in $V(2)$, and so on. $V(0)$ contains the length, 5, of V$.

The process can be reversed, too. The instruction:

CHANGE V TO V$

creates the string "HELLO" from the code numbers in V and stores it in V$. The zero'th item in V tells the computer how many code numbers should be changed back into characters.

The CHANGE statement can be used in various ways. Assume you wish to create a new string from two others stored in A$ and B$. At the present time, A$ = "BLACK" and B$ = "JACK"; the new string you want is "BLACK-JACK". Here is a program segment to create it:

```
50   CHANGE A$ TO X
52   CHANGE B$ TO Y
53   LET L1 = X(0)
55   FOR I = 1 TO Y(0)
57     LET L1 = L1 + 1
58     LET X(L1) = Y(I)
60   NEXT I
65   LET X(0) = X(0) + Y(0)
67   CHANGE X TO C$
70   PRINT "THE RESULTING STRING IS "; C$
71   STOP
```

2. The CHANGE statement is available only in systems that allow lists to have zero'th items.

Lines 50 and 52 change A\$ and B\$ into lists of code numbers; the code numbers for A\$ are stored in list X, and the code numbers for B\$ are stored in list Y. Since the contents of X(0) tell us A\$'s length, it is a simple matter to move the items in Y into list X, starting with the first "empty" item in X. And there are Y(0) items to move. After all the items in Y have been transferred to X, the only job remaining is to update X(0). Because we wish to create a new string containing the characters in A\$ followed by the characters in B\$, the length should equal $X(0) + Y(0)$. Therefore, line 65 assigns the value $(X(0) + Y(0))$ to X(0). The desired result is obtained by changing list X into string C\$.

Remember that the code numbers are numeric values; therefore, they may be manipulated like any other number. For example, if you want to ask whether the third character in V\$ is an "L," you could say:

$$IF\ V(3) = 76\ THEN\ 100$$

String Expressions

Expressions, as defined in chapter 2, may consist of a single variable or constant or any combination of variables and/or constants connected by operators. To be precise, anything meeting this description should be termed an *arithmetic expression*, since its evaluation by the computer will yield a numeric value.

Some expressions in BASIC do not meet the above description. In fact, they do not yield numeric values. One such type of expression is called a *string expression*. It may consist of one of the following:

1. an explicit string
2. a simple or subscripted string variable
3. a reference to a function having a string value

In the first instance, a string expression might consist of an explicit string like "ABC" or "PRESENT VALUE". Alternatively, a simple or subscripted string variable such as A\$, B\$(1), or Z\$(10,5) also qualifies as a bona fide string expression. Finally, string expressions may consist of functions having string values. We introduce this third instance in the next section of the chapter.

In most systems a string expression may not contain an operator and is, therefore, limited to one (and only one) of the three instances above. Things like A\$ * "XYZ" make no sense and are not legal string expressions for that reason; neither are things like (Q\$/X\$) * 10.5. All legal string expressions have two things in common: They contain no operators and they yield explicit strings, rather than numeric values, when evaluated.

String Functions

Some systems provide certain *string functions* that greatly enhance one's ability to manipulate strings of characters within a BASIC program.

The LEN function, for instance, yields a number equal to the length of the string given as an argument — i.e., inside the parentheses. For example:

LEN(A$)

causes the characters in the specific string to be counted and the resulting number substituted.[3] If A$ = "5 DOLLARS" then LEN(A$) = 9. Recall that blanks are important in strings, so they are included in the character count.

The general form of the LEN function is simply:

LEN(*string expression*)

Thus, you could say LEN(A$(23)) or LEN("ABRACADABRA"). And, you may use the LEN function wherever an arithmetic expression is legal, since the result is a numeric value. For example:

LET A9 = LEN(A$(5))
PRINT LEN(B$)
IF LEN("APPLE") > = LEN(W$) THEN 100
FOR I = 1 TO LEN (R$) STEP 2

Two string functions available on many systems allow you to convert numbers to strings and strings to numbers. The STR function, for instance, converts a number to a string containing the same digits. Its standard form is:

STR(*arithmetic expression*)

For example, STR(354) = "354", STR(5) = "5", and if J = 6, STR(J + 1) = "7". If the number contains a decimal point, so will the string: STR(12.5) = "12.5". Notice that, unlike LEN, the STR function has a string value; thus it is a legal string expression.

The VAL function does just the opposite: it converts a string of digits into a numeric value. The standard form is:

VAL(*string expression*)

For example, VAL("85") = 85, VAL("78.95") = 78.95, and if J$ = "15.8", VAL(J$) = 15.8. Just be careful not to use a string containing a non-numeric

---

3. In some systems, this function is referenced as LENGTH instead of LEN.

character with the VAL function—it would make no sense, and the computer would probably tell you so.

Another useful function is INDEX. It has the following form:[4]

INDEX (*string expression, string expression*)

Like the LEN and VAL functions, INDEX also yields a number. If the second string in the argument is part of the first, the value of the function is the position in the string being searched (specified by the first string expression) at which the searched-for string (specified by the second string expression) starts. If the second string is not part of the first, the value of the function is zero. For example, INDEX("ABC", "B") = 2. If A$ = "1543" and B$ = "75", then IN-DEX(A$,B$) = 0.

If the INDEX function yields a nonzero value, we say that the second string is a *substring* of the first. Thus, "JOHN" is a substring of "JOHNSON". But "JHSN" is not; a substring must represent consecutive characters. It also might occur more than once, as "O" does in "JOHNSON". If it does, INDEX will give you the position of the first occurrence. Since "O" occurs first as the second character, INDEX ("JOHNSON", "O") will equal 2.

Here is a sample program segment using INDEX:

```
300   LET C$ = "COLUMBUS"
310   PRINT "WHO DISCOVERED AMERICA ";
315   INPUT N$
320   IF INDEX(N$,C$) = 1 THEN 400
325   REM -- THERE'S STILL HOPE
330   IF INDEX(N$,"UMBUS") = 4 THEN 420
335   REM -- TRY ONCE MORE
340   IF INDEX(N$,"C") = 1 THEN 440
345   PRINT "TRY AGAIN.  HIS NAME BEGINS WITH C."
350   PRINT "WHO WAS HE";
355   GO TO 315
400   REM -- GOT IT RIGHT
410   PRINT "VERY GOOD."
415   GO TO 500
420   REM -- CLOSE
425   PRINT "THATS CLOSE.  ITS COLUMBUS."
430   GO TO 500
440   REM -- HE HAS THE RIGHT FIRST LETTER ANYWAY
445   PRINT "NOT QUITE, BUT THE FIRST LETTER IS"
450   PRINT "CORRECT AT LEAST.  TRY AGAIN."
455   GO TO 350
500   REM -- CONTINUE
```

In this case, INDEX was used to analyze a student's answer to the question: "Who discovered America?"

The SUBSTR(for substring) function is also extremely handy. With it you can create a new string that is a piece of an old one. It comes in two forms:

4. In some systems, the function name may be different; e.g., IDX or POS.

SUBSTR(*string expression, arithmetic expression*)

and

SUBSTR(*string expression, arithmetic expression, arithmetic expression*)

The string expression referenced in the first argument may, as our definition of string expressions suggests, be an explicit string, a simple or subscripted string variable, or a reference to another string-valued function (such as STR). Any arithmetic expression may be used for the second or third argument.

What does SUBSTR do? It creates substrings from existing strings. For example:

LET B$ = SUBSTR(A$,5)

This statement causes all the characters in A$ starting with the fifth one to be stored in B$. The first argument indicates the string from which a substring is to be created; the second tells which character of the original string is to be the first character of the substring.

Obviously, the SUBSTR function does not have a numeric value; it has a string value. SUBSTR("WILLIAM", 5) is equal to "IAM". And if A$ is equal to "HELLO", SUBSTR(A$, INDEX(A$,"L")) is equal to "LLO". Since it is legal to reference other string-valued functions in a string expression, it is perfectly acceptable to say SUBSTR(STR(123456789),4), in which case we obtain the string "456789".

The second form of SUBSTR allows you to create a substring from the middle of an existing string. For example, the statement:

LET C$ = SUBSTR("ABCDEF", 3,2)

is an instruction to: "Store in C$ a substring of "ABCDEF" which starts with the third character of the latter and has a length of 2." The third argument, if used, tells the computer how many characters the substring must have. In this case the string "CD" will be created.

There are many uses for SUBSTR. Here is a program segment to print a string with all its blanks removed:

```
10    FOR I = 1 TO LEN(S$)
20      LET T$ = SUBSTR(S$,I,1)
30      IF T$ = " " THEN 50
40      PRINT T$;
50    NEXT I
```

As another example, suppose you wish to have the user of your program input a string representing a date (such as "MAY 12, 1980"). Your goal is to obtain a substring containing only the day of the month (in this case, "12"). Here is one possibility:

```
100    PRINT "GIVE ME A DATE IN FORM:  MAY 12, 1980";
115    INPUT M$
120    LET C1 = INDEX(M$, " ")
125    LET C2 = INDEX(M$, ",") - C1 - 1
130    LET D$ = SUBSTR(M$,C1+1, C2)
135    PRINT "THE DAY OF THE MONTH IS "; D$
140    STOP
```

Some computer systems don't offer SUBSTR. In those cases, there may be other string functions that can be used to accomplish the same task. Two of the most useful are LEFT and RIGHT, defined as follows:

LEFT(*string expression, arithmetic expression*)

and

RIGHT(*string expression, arithmetic expression*)

Let's see how they work.

Suppose you have a string in W$ that equals "MORRIS FOXWORTHY", and you would like to create a new string that just equals "MORRIS". Noting that "MORRIS" has six characters and begins with the leftmost character position in W$, you can simply say:

LET X$ = LEFT(W$,6)

The result: After execution, X$ will equal "MORRIS". In general, the function LEFT first evaluates the arithmetic expression you give it as the second argument. That tells the computer how many characters you wish to extract from the left side of the string designated by the string expression of the first argument. Then, it simply creates the appropriate substring.

The RIGHT function works in an analogous fashion. If you now wish to create the substring "FOXWORTHY" you could say:

LET Y$ = RIGHT(W$,8)

which says, in effect, to place in Y$ the substring of W$ that starts with the eighth character and continues to the end. Since the "F" in "FOXWORTHY" occurs in the eighth position of W$, the desired result is obtained.

Both LEFT and RIGHT can be used in any statement where a string expression is allowed. Examples are:

IF LEFT(X$,3) = LEFT(Y$,3) THEN 540
PRINT RIGHT (E$(2,5),10)

LET S$ = LEFT(C$,1)
READ Y$(3,INT(VAL(RIGHT(C$,5))))

Just be sure whenever you use either function that the arithmetic expression you provide as the second argument has a whole number value; some computers will absolutely balk at anything else.

String Addition

On occasion, you may wish to append some characters to the end of an existing string. On many systems this is very simple. For example, to add the characters "ABC" to the right end of the string in C$, merely say:

LET C$ = C$ + "ABC"

The plus sign does not indicate normal addition; it is a notice to link two strings together. The procedure may be used to link several strings. For example:

LET R$ = "567" + SUBSTR(T$,3) + STR(A) + S$

Here, each string being linked may be referenced in the LET statement by a string expression; i.e., by an explicit string (such as "567"), by a string-valued function (such as SUBSTR(T$,3) or STR(A)), or by a string variable (such as S$). If the result is too long, of course, you may lose the rightmost characters.

In systems where string addition is not explicitly allowed, the CHANGE function can be used to do the same thing. The example on page 101 illustrated this possibility. Recall that CHANGE was used to create the string "BLACKJACK" from "BLACK" and "JACK". Although the use of CHANGE is somewhat awkward for this purpose, it is effective.

Problems

1. What is wrong with the following program (other than the fact that it is obviously nonsense)? (Assume the STR, SUBSTR, and VAL functions are available on this particular computer.)

```
10    DIM M$(100)
15    LET A$ = "123"
20    INPUT M$
25    LET B$ = 456
30    FOR I = 1 TO 100
35       FOR J = 0 TO 9
40          IF M$(I) = STR(J) THEN 60
45       NEXT J
```

```
47    NEXT I
50    PRINT M$; "CONTAINS NO DIGITS
53    STOP
60    LET C$ = VAL(A$)
62    LET D$ = STR(VAL(A$)/VAL(B$))
65    PRINT SUBSTR(A$,1,LENGTH(A$))
70    END
```

2. Modify the program on page 100 to alphabetize first and last names so that any blanks that may appear do not affect the ordering. (Assume SUBSTR, LEN, and string addition are legal.)

3. Using the CHANGE statement, write a subroutine that performs the INDEX function. Assume the string you are working with is in A$ and the substring you want to find is in B$.

4. A word is a *palindrome* if it is spelled the same backward and forward. Examples are: radar, level, pop. Using string functions, find out if the string currently in S$ is a palindrome.

5. A *binary search* procedure can be a very quick and efficient way to search a large alphabetical dictionary. Make up a list of at least ten words in alphabetical order. Then play computer and look for a particular word in it using the following program. How does a binary search work?

```
10    PRINT "HOW MANY WORDS IN YOUR DICTIONARY ";
12    INPUT N
15    REM -- READ DICTIONARY
17    FOR I = 1 TO N
19      INPUT S$(I)
20    NEXT I
21    LET R1 = 1
22    LET R2 = N
23    LET R3 = 0
25    PRINT "WHAT IS YOUR WORD ";
30    INPUT T$
32    LET R4 = INT((R1 + R2)/2 + .5)
33    IF R4 = R3 THEN 80
34    LET R3 = R4
40    IF S$(R3) = T$ THEN 70
43    IF S$(R3) > T$ THEN 60
50    REM -- NOT FAR ENOUGH IN LIST
53    LET R1 = R3
55    GO TO 32
60    REM -- TOO FAR DOWN
62    LET R2 = R3
64    GO TO 32
70    REM -- STRING FOUND
75    PRINT "YOUR WORD IS IN THE DICTIONARY."
77    GO TO 21
80    REM -- IT MAY NOT BE HERE
82    IF S$(R3 - 1) = T$ THEN 70
83    PRINT "SORRY, ITS NOT HERE."
85    GO TO 21
90    END
```

6. You have just been hired by a corporation to think up names for its many new products. The president has given you the following rule: All proposed

names must have five letters, begin with a consonant, and be composed of alternating consonants and vowels. Program a "random name" generator that conforms to this rule. Note: You may use string functions, but they are not necessary.

To complete problem 7 and 8 below, use string features that are available on your computer. Check your computer's reference manual before proceeding.

7. Write a program to accept a series of words from someone at a computer terminal. As each new word is input, place it in its proper alphabetical order in a list. Start off with an empty list, add each new word alphabetically, and weed out any duplicates that might arise. When the user has given you the last word, he or she will input "BYE". Then print out the list.

8. Write a program to read in a list of telephone numbers in string form, e.g., "206-554-2121" or "714-882-9956". The first three digits of each number represent the area code, the next two the prefix, etc. Sort the numbers into three groups: those outside the "206" area (these are long-distance calls from Washington State), those inside the "206" area but having any prefixes other than "55," "32," or "62" (these are toll calls for certain people who live in Washington), and all other numbers. Assume there are 100 strings in all. Print out each group of strings separately.

Answers

1. Line 20: This may not be illegal, but M$ has previously been defined as a list; it is a good idea to avoid using it as a simple string variable.

   Line 25: Illegal in most systems. A string variable should not be assigned a numeric value.

   Line 40: This is okay. J is an expression; therefore, it is correct to say STR(J).

   Line 50: This will cause an error. The programmer forgot the quotation mark after the word "DIGITS".

   Line 60: VAL(A$) is equal to 123. So far, so good. But C$ is a string variable and should not be used to hold a number.

   Line 62: Nothing wrong here. VAL(A$)/VAL(B$) is an expression and may therefore be used as the argument for the STR function.

   Line 65: Perfectly acceptable, but an inefficient way to print A$.

2. A simple way to do this is to create two new string lists, say, V$ and H$. Let these two lists hold the original first and last names, while F$ and W$ are used to hold the names with all the blanks removed. Comparisons are done using F$ and W$, but when switches are made they are made to V$ and H$ as well. Here is the method:

```
50    REM -- SORT FIRST AND LAST NAME
55    FOR I = 1 TO 100
57    LET V$(I) = W$(I)
60    LET H$(I) = F$(I)
62    NEXT I
65    REM -- NOW REMOVE BLANKS FROM W$ AND F$
67    GOSUB 300
68    LET S = 0
70    FOR I = 1 TO 99
80    IF W$(I) = W$(I+1) THEN 180
90    IF W$(I) < W$(I+1) THEN 230
100   LET S = S + 1
110   LET Z$ = W$(I)
120   LET X$ = F$(I)
130   LET W$(I) = W$(I+1)
140   LET F$(I) = F$(I+1)
150   LET W$(I+1) = Z$
160   LET F$(I+1) = X$
162   LET Z$ = V$(I)
164   LET X$ = H$(I)
166   LET V$(I) = V$(I+1)
168   LET V$(I+1) = Z$
170   LET H$(I) = H$(I+1)
172   LET H$(I+1) = X$
175   GO TO 230
180   IF F$(I) <= F$(I+1) THEN 230
190   LET S = S + 1
200   LET Z$ = F$(I)
210   LET F$(I) = F$(I+1)
220   LET F$(I+1) = X$
222   LET Z$ = H$(I)
224   LET H$(I) = H$(I+1)
226   LET H$(I+1) = Z$
230   NEXT I
240   IF S > 0 THEN 68
250   REM -- SORT IS COMPLETED
```

Subroutine 300, which removes the blanks from lists W$ and F$, might look like this:

```
300   REM -- REMOVE THE BLANKS FROM LISTS W$ AND F$
310   FOR I = 1 TO 100
320   LET T = 0
330   FOR J = 1 TO LEN(W$(I))
335   IF SUBSTR(W$(I),J,1) = " " THEN 370
340   IF T <> 0 THEN 360
345   LET T = 1
350   LET Q$ = SUBSTR(W$(I),J,1)
355   GO TO 370
360   LET Q$ = Q$ + SUBSTR(W$(I),J,1)
370   NEXT J
375   LET W$(I) =Q$
380   LET T = 0
385   FOR J = 1 TO LEN(F$(I))
387   IF SUBSTR(F$(I),J,1) = " " THEN 450
390   IF T <> 0 THEN 420
395   LET T = 1
400   LET Q$ = SUBSTR(F$(I),J,1)
410   GO TO 450
420   LET Q$ = Q$ + SUBSTR(F$(I),J,1)
450   NEXT J
460   LET F$(I) = Q$
465   NEXT I
470   RETURN
```

3. Here is one method:

```
200    REM -- INDEX SUBROUTINE
201    REM -- A$ IS STRING, B$ MAY BE SUBSTRING
202    REM -- I1 IS INDEX(A$,B$)
205    CHANGE A$ TO A
207    CHANGE B$ TO B
210    FOR I1 = 1 TO (A(0)-B(0)+1)
212      LET J1 = I1
214      FOR J = 1 TO B(0)
215        IF A(J1) <> B(J) THEN 230
216        LET J1 = J1 + 1
218      NEXT J
220    REM -- B$ IS A SUBSTRING
221    RETURN
230    NEXT I1
232    REM -- B$ IS NOT A SUBSTRING
233    LET I1 = 0
235    RETURN
```

4.

```
10    LET C1 = LENGTH(S$)
13    FOR I = 1 TO INT(C1/2)
15      IF SUBSTR(S$,I,1) <> SUBSTR(S$,C1-I+1,1) THEN 30
17    NEXT I
20    PRINT S$; " IS A PALINDROME "
22    GO TO 32
30    PRINT S$; " IS NOT A PALINDROME "
32    REM -- CONTINUE
```

6. This is one approach.

```
10    REM -- RANDOM NAME GENERATOR
12    DIM C$(21), V$(5)
13    REM -- READ CONSONANTS
15    FOR I = 1 TO 21
17      READ C$(I)
20    NEXT I
21    REM -- READ VOWELS
22    FOR I = 1 TO 5
25      READ V$(I)
27    NEXT I
30    REM -- GENERATE 100 NAMES
31    FOR I = 1 TO 100
32      GOSUB 100
33      PRINT C$(R1); V$(R2)
34      GOSUB 100
35      PRINT C$(R1);V$(R2)
37      GOSUB 100
39      PRINT C$(R1)
40    NEXT I
50    STOP
100   REM -- GENERATE RANDOM NUMBERS
101   LET R1 = INT(RND*21 + 1)
102   LET R2 = INT(RND*5 + 1)
103   RETURN
```

And here are the data:

```
900    REM -- DATA FOR RANDOM NAME GENERATOR
901    DATA "B","C","D","F","G","H","J","K","L"
902    DATA "M","N","P","Q","R","S","T","V","W"
903    DATA "X","Y","Z"
904    DATA "A","E","I","O","U"
910    END
```

7. You're on your own. Good luck.

8. Some useful functions for solving this problem include RIGHT, LEFT, VAL, SUBSTR, INDEX, and/or CHANGE. Tailor your approach to the functions that are permitted on your system.

CHAPTER 10

String Applications

Many routine tasks require the ability to process string data. This is readily apparent in the business world, for instance, where firms frequently process alphabetic information including customer names and addresses, employee names, product descriptions, shipping information, and the like. These data also must be routinely maintained on files, with old items deleted, new items added, and changes made periodically to still other items. For these purposes, computer programs that manipulate strings are indispensable.

This chapter presents two string application programs that might be useful to a business firm. They were written for a specific computer system that accepts the SUBSTR, LEN, VAL, and STR functions, but that does not allow INDEX, LEFT, RIGHT, or string addition. Therefore, you may wish to modify them to suit the requirements of your computer system.

Computer-generated Form Letters

Ever wonder how those "personalized" form letters that are sent out by various organizations to advertise sweepstakes contests and the like are generated? Undoubtedly, you or someone you know has received a few such letters, as they are becoming increasingly common. Recall that these letters usually mention your name or some other piece of personal information within the body of the letter. If your name were John Smith, for instance, a hypothetical letter might read:

Mr. John Smith
333 N. E. 34th Street
Janesville, Wisconsin 45678

Dear Mr. Smith:

Congratulations, Mr. Smith, you could already be a winner in our 50th annual Grand Sweepstakes Competition! Over 200 other families in Wisconsin have been lucky in the past, and now it is *your* turn to win an all-expense paid tour of Milpitas, California, for your family!

All you have to do, Mr. Smith, is to . . .

And so it goes. When you think about it, those letters are very likely to be computer-generated. It is easy to instruct a computer to insert different pieces of "personalized" information into the body of a standard text and then print thousands of letters, each with the appearance of having been written just for the recipient. Let's see how we might write a BASIC program to do just that.

Suppose the owner of a business firm wishes to send letters periodically to its customers as part of a marketing strategy. Imagine that there are two basic types of letters. The first — which we shall call type A — is to be sent each time an existing customer tries a new product sold by the firm. This letter might be used to encourage the customer to keep buying the product in the future. The second letter — type B — would be sent, instead, whenever a customer has experienced problems with a defective product. In this instance, the firm wishes to express its apologies and to pledge that this will not happen again.

The owner suggests that letter A should read something like this:

Mr. Morris Foxworthy
88 Gateway Lane
New York, New York 11111

Dear Mr. Foxworthy:

We are so happy you have decided to try our product E-Z-Flow. Ever since 1959 when you first became a customer of ours, Mr. Foxworthy, we have hoped you would get to know this fabulous pancake syrup.

Congratulations for trying the product we recommend as the pancake syrup of all pancake syrups.

Sincerely,

In order to design a BASIC program to produce this letter, it is necessary to identify the specific pieces of information that are different for each customer to whom the letter is sent.

We might rewrite letter A in skeleton form, indicating with blanks where customer-specific information will be inserted. This gives:

(title, first and last name)
(address)
- •
- •
- •
(address)

Dear *(title and last name):*

We are so happy you have decided to try our product *(name of product)*. Ever since *(year)* when you first became a customer of ours *(title and last name)*, we have hoped you would get to know this fabulous *(type of product)*.

Congratulations for trying the product we recommend as the *(type of product)* of all *(type of product)*s.

Sincerely,

As you can see, the necessary pieces of customer information are the following:

1. The customer's title, first and last names.
2. The customer's address.
3. The name of the product he or she purchased.
4. The type of product purchased (product description).
5. The year in which the individual first became a customer of the firm.

Now let's look at letter B to determine its information requirements. Letter B is like A — short. The owner suggests that it read as follows:

Ms. Wanda Wilkie
459 Park Hills Road
Alexandria, Virginia 22222

Dear Ms. Wilkie:

We are so sorry about the problems you have recently experienced with our product Mor-Score. Ever since 1974 when you first became a customer of ours, Ms. Wilkie, we have vowed to provide you with the best possible flyswatter.

We will do everything we can in the future to see that you receive satisfaction with this high-quality flyswatter.

Sincerely,

Again, we must identify those items that will be varied with each letter sent. Here, then, is letter B in skeleton form:

(title, first and last name)
(address)
- •
- •
- •

(address)

Dear *(title and last name):*

We are so sorry about the problems you have recently experienced with our product *(name of product)*. Ever since *(year)* when you first became a customer of ours *(title and name)*, we have vowed to provide you with the best possible *(type of product)*.

We will do everything we can in the future to see that you receive satisfaction with this high quality *(type of product)*.

Sincerely,

As shown, this letter requires the same five pieces of information required for letter A. Hence, both letter types can easily be incorporated into one BASIC program.

The following pages show the program we wrote to generate letters A and B. In lines 10-60 of the program, the user (e.g., an office employee) is directed to input the five basic pieces of information concerning each letter to be typed. The computer prompts the user by indicating what piece of information is to be provided at each stage. For instance, the computer first (in lines 20-24) asks:

> TO WHOM IS THIS LETTER TO BE SENT?
> PLEASE GIVE TITLE AND FIRST NAME—
> EXAMPLE: MS. SALLY
> THEN GIVE LAST NAME—EXAMPLE: JONES
> TITLE AND FIRST NAME?

After the last line above, the user should input the customer's title and first name. Upon storing the response in N$, the computer then says:

> LAST NAME?

to which the user responds by typing in the customer's last name (line 32). This is stored in L$. Notice that since the computer accepts a maximum of 18 characters per string, the use of two string variables for the customer's entire name is desirable. Otherwise, many individuals' names might have to be drastically abbreviated.

```
10      REM -- PROGRAM TO PRINT FORM LETTERS.  USER INPUTS
11      REM -- INFORMATION CONCERNING THE TYPE OF LETTER TO
12      REM -- BE SENT, TO WHOM IT IS TO BE SENT, AND PRODUCT
13      REM -- INFORMATION.
20      PRINT "TO WHOM IS THIS LETTER TO BE SENT?"
21      PRINT "PLEASE GIVE TITLE AND FIRST NAME--";
22      PRINT "EXAMPLE: MS. SALLY"
23      PRINT "THEN GIVE LAST NAME--EXAMPLE: JONES"
24      PRINT "TITLE AND FIRST NAME";
25      INPUT N$
28      GOSUB 300
29      IF T <> 0 THEN 24
31      PRINT "LAST NAME";
32      INPUT L$
33      PRINT "HOW MANY LINES IN THE ADDRESS";
35      INPUT A
36      PRINT "PLEASE ENTER EACH LINE OF ADDRESS SEPARATELY."
37      PRINT "LIMIT EACH LINE TO A MAXIMUM OF 18 CHARACTERS."
40      FOR I = 1 TO A
42        INPUT A$(I)
45      NEXT I
48      PRINT "HOW LONG HAS "; N$; " "; L$; " BEEN A CUSTOMER?"
49      PRINT "EXAMPLE: SINCE 1972"
50      INPUT R$
52      PRINT "WHAT PRODUCT DID "; N$; " "; L$; " PURCHASE";
54      INPUT P$
55      PRINT "WHAT TYPE OF PRODUCT IS IT"
60      INPUT T$
70      REM -- ASK FOR TYPE OF LETTER TO BE SENT, THEN PRINT IT
71      PRINT "WHICH LETTER DO YOU WISH TO SEND--"
72      PRINT "TYPE A--CONGRATULATIONS FOR TRYING PRODUCT"
73      PRINT "TYPE B--WE ARE SORRY ABOUT PRODUCT"
74      PRINT "INPUT ONE LETTER--A OR B";
75      INPUT E$
77      FOR I = 1 TO 10
78      PRINT
79      NEXT I
80      REM -- LOOK FOR FIRST BLANK IN N$
81      LET W$ - " "
82      LET Q$ = N$
83      GOSUB 400
84      IF T <> 0 THEN 90
85      REM -- IF NO BLANK, LOOK FOR PERIOD
86      LET W$ = "."
87      GOSUB 400
90      LET S$ = SUBSTR(N$,1,T)
91      PRINT N$; " "; L$
93      FOR I = 1 TO A
95        PRINT A$(I)
96      NEXT I
97      PRINT
98      PRINT "DEAR "; S$; " "; L$
99      PRINT
100     REM -- DETERMINE WHICH LETTER TO BE TYPED
102     IF E$ <> "A" THEN 200
104     PRINT "WE ARE SO HAPPY YOU HAVE DECIDED TO TRY OUR PRODUCT ";
106     PRINT P$;"."
109     PRINT "EVER "; R$; " WHEN YOU FIRST BECAME A CUSTOMER ";
110     PRINT "OF OURS,"
120     PRINT S$; " "; L$; ", WE HAVE HOPED YOU WOULD GET TO KNOW THIS"
121     PRINT "FABULOUS ";T$; "."
122     PRINT
124     PRINT "CONGRATULATIONS FOR TRYING THE PRODUCT WE ";
125     PRINT "RECOMMEND AS THE "
126     PRINT T$; " OF ALL "; T$; "S."
127     PRINT
128     PRINT "SINCERELY,"
129     PRINT
130     PRINT
132     STOP
```

```
200    REM -- PRINT LETTER TYPE B
210    PRINT "WE ARE SO SORRY ABOUT THE PROBLEMS YOU HAVE RECENTLY";
220    PRINT "EXPERIENCED WITH "
230    PRINT "OUR PRODUCT "; P$; ". EVER "; R$; " WHEN YOU FIRST ";
235    PRINT "BECAME A "
240    PRINT "CUSTOMER OF OURS, "; S$; " "; L$; " WE HAVE VOWED ";
245    PRINT "TO PROVIDE"
250    PRINT "YOU WITH THE BEST POSSIBLE "; T$; "."
251    PRINT
260    PRINT "WE WILL DO EVERYTHING WE CAN IN THE FUTURE TO SEE ";
262    PRINT "THAT YOU RECEIVE"
265    PRINT "SATISFACTION WITH THIS HIGH-QUALITY "; T$; "."
270    GO TO 127
300    REM -- SUBROUTINE TO CHECK FOR PRESENCE OF TITLE
310    LET T = 0
312    IF SUBSTR(N$,1,4) = "MRS." THEN 350
315    IF SUBSTR(N$,1,4) = "MISS" THEN 350
318    IF SUBSTR(N$,1,3) = "MR." THEN 350
320    IF SUBSTR(N$,1,3) = "MS." THEN 350
324    IF SUBSTR(N$,1,3) = "DR." THEN 350
328    IF SUBSTR(N$,1,6) = "MASTER" THEN 350
330    IF SUBSTR(N$,1,9) = "PROFESSOR" THEN 350
335    REM -- TITLE IS ASSUMED TO BE MISSING
340    PRINT "CUSTOMER'S TITLE IS MISSING."
342    PRINT "PLEASE INPUT TITLE AND FIRST NAME AGAIN."
345    LET T = 1
350    RETURN
400    REM -- SUBROUTINE TO SCAN A STRING FOR A CHARACTER
401    FOR I = 1 TO LEN(Q$)
403      IF SUBSTR(Q$,I,1) <> W$ THEN 420
405      LET T = I
410    RETURN
420    NEXT I
425    LET T = 0
427    RETURN
500    END
```

Notice that after N$ has been filled, the computer branches (in line 28) to subroutine 300 in order to check that string for the presence of the customer's title. It scans N$ for one of the following titles: MRS., MISS, MR., MS., DR., MASTER, or PROFESSOR. For this purpose, the SUBSTR function is used to compare each of the above titles to the first few characters of N$. If no match to any of these titles is found, the computer assumes that the title was not provided and instructs the user to re-input the data in N$. It is generally a good idea in a "production" program of this sort to double-check the correctness of data provided by the user. Typographical errors and/or omissions are not uncommon, and they can be very costly if they go undetected.

The customer's address presents one small problem. Some individuals require only one- or two-line addresses, while others may require four or five lines. For instance, some addresses may be very short:

P. O. Box 85
Houston TX 22222

while others may be very long:

c/o Ace Office Supply
Pencil Division
2367 East Arbor Drive
Suite 3F
Seattle WA 33333

Hence, in line 33 the computer asks the user to indicate how many lines make up the customer's address. The number that is input (and stored in A) is used as the terminal value for variable I in the FOR-NEXT loop that begins on line 40. At this point (lines 36–37), the computer types:

PLEASE ENTER EACH LINE OF ADDRESS SEPARATELY.
LIMIT EACH LINE TO A MAXIMUM OF 18 CHARACTERS.
?

As each question mark appears, the user types in the next line of the address, until all the lines have been entered. (Obviously, none of the lines should contain an embedded comma; otherwise, the computer will think the user has input two strings for a given line instead of the one that is sought.)[1]

Finally, in lines 48-60, the computer asks for information relating to the length of time the addressee has been a customer (R$), the specific product purchased (P$), and the type of product (T$). With all of this information now available, the computer asks (in lines 71–74) for the type of letter to be sent:

WHICH LETTER DO YOU WISH TO SEND—
TYPE A—CONGRATULATIONS FOR TRYING PRODUCT
TYPE B—WE ARE SORRY ABOUT PRODUCT
INPUT ONE LETTER—A OR B?

The user responds to the question mark with the appropriate letter, which is stored in E$.

In lines 77-99, the computer formats the customer's address and salutation on the printed page. Notice that it makes use of subroutine 400 to search for the last character of the customer's title in N$. The subroutine functions as the INDEX function would, were it available on this system. Specifically, subroutine 400 scans a given string (Q$) for the first occurrence of a single character (W$). The first time the computer goes to the subroutine (from line 83), Q$ is set equal to N$ and W$ is a one-character "blank" string. If, upon returning from the subroutine, the computer finds that variable T equals zero, no blank

---

1. In some systems embedded commas can be included if the line is typed with quotation marks.

was found in Q\$. Otherwise, T will contain the location of the first blank in Q\$. If T = 0, subroutine 400 is called again, this time with W\$ equal to a period ("."). The occurrence of either character in N\$ is assumed to mean that everything before (and including) that character is part of the customer's title, while everything following that character is part of the customer's proper name. This *parsing* (separating out the components) of N\$ is necessary because the salutation of the letter should not include the customer's first name, but should include his or her title. It would be quite inappropriate, for instance, to have a salutation that read:

DEAR DR. MAYBELLE WASHBURN:

instead of:

DEAR DR. WASHBURN:

Thus, a substring of N\$ is created (line 90) that starts with the first character of N\$ and includes all characters up through the T'th (where T indicates the location of the first period or blank). This substring is placed in S\$, so that to print the salutation, the computer executes the command:

98   PRINT "DEAR"; S\$"; " "; L\$

When it reaches line 102, the computer determines whether E\$ is equal to "A" or "B." If it equals an "A," the computer prints the text of letter A (lines 104–130); otherwise, it prints the text of letter B (lines 200–270). The printing of each letter is very simple. The portion of the letter that is "boilerplate" (the same for each customer) is generated by using literal strings in the PRINT commands; whenever unique customer information is to be interjected, however, the appropriate string variable is printed. What could be easier?

The following shows one example for each type of letter. For clarity, the information input by the user has been underlined. If desired, the program can be modified so that it prints mailing labels as well. Then only the signatures would have to be entered manually.

```
TO WHOM IS THIS LETTER TO BE SENT?
PLEASE GIVE TITLE AND FIRST NAME -- EXAMPLE: MS. SALLY
THEN GIVE LAST NAME -- EXAMPLE: JONES
TITLE AND FIRST NAME ? MS. MAUDE
LAST NAME ?MADHATTER
HOW MANY LINES IN THE ADDRESS ?2
PLEASE ENTER EACH LINE OF ADDRESS SEPARATELY.
LIMIT EACH LINE TO A MAXIMUM OF 18 CHARACTERS.
?44 FERN LANE
?MILPITAS CA 54321
HOW LONG HAS MS. MAUDE MADHATTER BEEN A CUSTOMER?
```

```
EXAMPLE: SINCE 1972
?SINCE 1947
WHAT PRODUCT DID MS. MAUDE MADHATTER PURCHASE ?FOAMIES
WHAT TYPE OF PRODUCT IS IT
?FOOTPAD
WHICH LETTER DO YOU WISH TO SEND--
TYPE A -- CONGRATULATIONS FOR TRYING PRODUCT
TYPE B -- WE ARE SORRY ABOUT PRODUCT
INPUT ONE LETTER -- A OR B ? A
```

```
MS. MAUDE MADHATTER
44 FERN LANE
MILPITAS CA 54321

DEAR MS. MADHATTER

WE ARE SO HAPPY YOU HAVE DECIDED TO TRY OUR PRODUCT FOAMIES.
EVER SINCE 1947 WHEN YOU FIRST BECAME A CUSTOMER OF OURS,
MS. MADHATTER, WE HAVE HOPED YOU WOULD GET TO KNOW THIS
FABULOUS FOOTPAD.

CONGRATULATIONS FOR TRYING THE PRODUCT WE RECOMMEND AS THE
FOOTPAD OF ALL FOOTPADS.

SINCERELY,
```

```
TO WHOM IS THIS LETTER TO BE SENT?
PLEASE GIVE TITLE AND FIRST NAME -- EXAMPLE: MS. SALLY
THEN GIVE LAST NAME -- EXAMPLE: JONES
TITLE AND FIRST NAME ? DR. WALTER P.
LAST NAME ?BUNCZAK
HOW MANY LINES IN THE ADDRESS ?3
PLEASE ENTER EACH LINE OF ADDRESS SEPARATELY.
LIMIT EACH LINE TO A MAXIMUM OF 18 CHARACTERS.
?245 ROYAL COURT
?APARTMENT F
?MADISON WI 12345
HOW LONG HAS DR. WALTER P. BUNCZAK BEEN A CUSTOMER?
EXAMPLE: SINCE 1972
?SINCE 1899
WHAT PRODUCT DID DR. WALTER P. BUNCZAK PURCHASE ?BUBBLIES
WHAT TYPE OF PRODUCT IS IT
?BUBBLE BATH
WHICH LETTER DO YOU WISH TO SEND--
TYPE A -- CONGRATULATIONS FOR TRYING PRODUCT
TYPE B -- WE ARE SORRY ABOUT PRODUCT
INPUT ONE LETTER -- A OR B ? B
```

```
DR. WALTER P. BUNCZAK
245 ROYAL COURT
APARTMENT F
MADISON WI   12345

DEAR DR. BUNCZAK

WE ARE SO SORRY ABOUT THE PROBLEMS YOU HAVE RECENTLY EXPERIENCED WITH
OUR PRODUCT BUBBLIES.  EVER SINCE 1899 WHEN YOU FIRST BECAME A
```

```
CUSTOMER OF OURS, DR.  BUNCZAK WE HAVE VOWED TO PROVIDE
YOU WITH THE BEST POSSIBLE BUBBLE BATH.

WE WILL DO EVERYTHING WE CAN IN THE FUTURE TO SEE THAT YOU RECEIVE
SATISFACTION WITH THIS HIGH-QUALITY BUBBLE BATH.

SINCERELY,
```

A Check-Writing Program

In the business world, a great many checks are written. These include payroll checks, checks written in payment to creditors and suppliers, pension checks, refund checks, and checks written to pay taxes and other fees. Consequently, many businesses use computers to perform such routine tasks as entering the information appearing on individual checks. Special automatically feeding check forms can be placed on an output device (such as a printer or terminal) for this purpose. In this way, much manual and clerical effort is eliminated.

How might a program that instructs the computer to write checks be designed? The program shown on the following pages offers a concrete example. It allows the employee using the computer to input the data necessary to write up to 100 different checks. Then, presuming that the computer's output device has been supplied with the appropriate blank check forms, the program prints out each one. The only tasks left to humans are the physical signing and mailing of the checks. Let's see how the program operates.

At the beginning of the program, certain housekeeping tasks are performed. For example, lines 10–35 in the listing serve to dimension several lists that will be employed in printing checks and to initialize two lists (S$ and R$) to contain certain string constants. (These lists will be discussed later.) Lines 37–87 then instruct the user to input the information necessary to print each check. First, the computer asks (line 37):

WHAT IS THE CURRENT DATE
(EXAMPLE: DECEMBER 12 1978)?

This information is printed at the top of every check. Note that because the date is stored in a single string variable (D$), it should not contain an embedded comma.[2]

After the user provides the date, the computer then asks (lines 40–42):

---

2. Unless entered within quotation marks (if possible).

```
10    REM -- COMPUTER CHECK PRINTING PROGRAM
11    REM -- ENTER NAMES, DOLLAR AMOUNTS FOR UP TO
12    REM -- ONE HUNDRED CHECKS.  COMPUTER WRITES
13    REM -- OUT EACH CHECK.
20    DIM S$(19), R$(8), F$(100), L$(100), A$(100), V(100)
25    REM -- INITIALIZE LISTS
27    FOR I = 1 TO 19
28    READ S$(I)
29    NEXT I
30    FOR I = 1 TO 8
32    READ R$(I)
35    NEXT I
37    PRINT "WHAT IS THE CURRENT DATE"
38    PRINT "(EXAMPLE: DECEMBER 12 1978)"
39    PRINT D$
40    PRINT "WHAT IS THE NAME OF YOUR COMPANY";
42    INPUT B$
43    PRINT "HOW MANY CHECKS DO YOU WISH TO PRINT";
44    INPUT N
45    IF N <= 100 THEN 50
46    PRINT "I CAN PRINT ONLY 100 CHECKS AT A TIME. TRY AGAIN."
47    GO TO 43
50    PRINT "WITH WHAT CHECK NUMBER DO YOU WISH TO START";
52    INPUT C
54    REM -- NOW INPUT INFORMATION FOR EACH CHECK
55    PRINT "FOR EACH CHECK, PLEASE PROVIDE THE FOLLOWING "
57    PRINT "INFORMATION: (EXAMPLE OF DOLLAR AMOUNT: $23402.50"
58    PRINT "THE MAXIMUM VALUE IS $999999.99)"
59    PRINT
60    FOR I = 1 TO N
62    PRINT "CHECK NUMBER "; I + C - 1
65    PRINT "LAST NAME";
66    INPUT L$(I)
67    PRINT "FIRST NAME";
68    INPUT F$(I)
69    PRINT "DOLLAR AMOUNT";
70    INPUT A$(I)
71    GOSUB 300
72    IF F = 0 THEN 78
73    PRINT "ERROR, TRY AGAIN"
74    GO TO 69
78    PRINT
79    PRINT
80    NEXT I
85    FOR J = 1 TO 5
86    PRINT
87    NEXT J

90    REM -- NOW PRINT INDIVIDUAL ITEMS
95    FOR I = 1 TO N
99    FOR K = 1 TO 72
100   PRINT "-";
105   NEXT K
107   PRINT
108   PRINT "CHECK NUMBER "; I + C - 1; TAB(50); D$
109   PRINT
110   PRINT "PAY TO THE ORDER OF....."; F$(I); " "; L$(I);
112   LET R = 33 - LEN(F$(I)) - LEN(L$(I))
113   IF R <= 0 THEN 120
115   FOR K = 1 TO R
116   PRINT ".";
118   NEXT K
120   PRINT TAB(60); "$"; A$(I)
125   PRINT
126   PRINT TAB(5);
170   REM -- NOW PRINT THE CHECK
172   IF INT(VAL(A$(I))) < 1000 THEN 230
173   LET T = LEN(STR(INT(VAL(A$(I))))) - 3
174   LET X$ = SUBSTR(A$(I),1,T)
175   GOSUB 500
```

```
178     PRINT " THOUSAND";
180     REM -- AMOUNT LESS THAN ONE THOUSAND
182     IF V(I) <> 0 THEN 185
183     LET X$ = SUBSTR(A$(I), T + 1, LEN(A$(I)))
184     GO TO 190
185     LET X$ = SUBSTR(A$(I), T+1, V(I)-T-1)
190     GOSUB 500
192     PRINT " AND";
200     REM -- AMOUNT IS IN CENTS
205     IF V(I) <> 0 THEN 215
211     PRINT " "; "00/100 DOLLARS"
212     GO TO 217
215     LET X$ = SUBSTR(A$(I), V(I)+1)
216     PRINT " "; X$; "/100 DOLLARS"
217     PRINT
218     PRINT TAB(20); "SIGNED--"
219     PRINT TAB(30)
220     FOR K = 1 TO LEN(B$)
221     PRINT SUBSTR(B$, K, 1); " ";
222     NEXT K
223     PRINT
224     NEXT I
225     FOR K = 1 TO 72
226     PRINT "-";
227     NEXT K
228     STOP
230     LET T = LEN(STR(INT(VAL(A$(I)))))
232     LET X$ = SUBSTR(A$(I), 1, T)
234     GO TO 190
300     REM -- SUBROUTINE TO CHECK FOR ERRORS IN AMOUNT
310     REM -- STRIP OFF DOLLAR SIGN FIRST
320     LET F = 0
328     IF SUBSTR(A$(I), 1, 1) <> "$" THEN 330
329     LET A$(I) = SUBSTR(A$(I), 2)
330     LET Y$ = A$(I)
331     LET N$ = "."
332     GOSUB 400
334     LET V(I) = T
339     IF V(I) = 0 THEN 360
340     IF LEN(A$(I)) <= 9 THEN 370
342     LET F = 1
344     RETURN
360     IF LEN(A$(I)) <= 6 THEN 370
362     LET F = 1
365     RETURN
370     REM -- NO ERRORS FOUND
372     RETURN
400     REM -- SUBROUTINE TO LOOK FOR THE FIRST OCCURRENCE OF A
410     REM -- SINGLE CHARACTER IN STRING Y$
412     REM -- LOCATION OF CHARACTER IN Y$ IS STORED IN T
413     REM -- INITIALIZE VARIABLE T FIRST
415     LET T = 0
420     FOR K = 1 TO LEN(Y$)
422     IF N$ <> SUBSTR(Y$, K, 1) THEN 440
424     LET T = K
425     RETURN
440     NEXT K
450     RETURN
500     REM -- SUBROUTINE TO PRINT DOLLAR AMOUNTS
510     LET J = VAL(SUBSTR(X$,1,1))
515     LET K = VAL(X$)
520     IF K <> 0 THEN 530
522     RETURN
530     ON LEN(X$) GO TO 550, 570, 590
535     STOP
550     PRINT " "; S$(J);
555     RETURN
570     IF K >= 20 THEN 580
575     PRINT " "; S$(K);
578     RETURN
580     IF VAL(SUBSTR(X$,2)) = 0 THEN 585
582     PRINT " "; R$(J-1); "-"; S$(VAL(SUBSTR(X$,2)));
```

```
583    RETURN
585    PRINT " "; R$(J-1);
588    RETURN
590    IF J = 0 THEN 595
592    PRINT " "; S$(J); " HUNDRED";
595    IF VAL(SUBSTR(X$,2,1)) = 0 THEN 598
596    PRINT " "; R$(VAL(SUBSTR(X$,2,1))-1);
598    IF VAL(SUBSTR(X$,3)) = 0 THEN 600
599    PRINT "-"; S$(VAL(SUBSTR(X$,3)));
600    RETURN
700    DATA "ONE", "TWO", "THREE", "FOUR", "FIVE"
701    DATA "SIX", "SEVEN", "EIGHT", "NINE", "TEN"
702    DATA "ELEVEN", "TWELVE", "THIRTEEN", "FOURTEEN",
703    DATA "FIFTEEN", "SIXTEEN", "SEVENTEEN", "EIGHTEEN"
704    DATA "NINETEEN"
800    DATA "TWENTY", "THIRTY", "FORTY", "FIFTY"
801    DATA "SIXTY", "SEVENTY", "EIGHTY", "NINETY"
900    END
```

WHAT IS THE NAME OF YOUR COMPANY?

In this case, the company name is that of the payor, i.e., the owner of the checking account on which each check will be drawn. This name is printed at the bottom of every check as a means of identification. The user should respond to this question with a string (to be stored in B$) not exceeding 18 characters.

The next question asked (lines 43–44) is:

HOW MANY CHECKS DO YOU WISH TO PRINT?

A valid response to this question must be a number less than or equal to 100. If the number input (which is stored in variable N) is greater than 100 (see line 45), the computer responds:

I CAN PRINT ONLY 100 CHECKS AT A TIME. TRY AGAIN.

and returns to line 43.

Another necessary piece of information is the check number with which the program should begin the sequence of checks printed. If you have your own checking account, you are aware that each check you write has a preprinted, unique sequence number. This numbering system allows you, among other things, to determine readily which checks are missing from the batch that has been cashed and returned to you with your bank statement each month. It is important to maintain the numeric sequence with each new set of checks written. This is why the computer asks (lines 50–52):

WITH WHAT CHECK NUMBER DO YOU WISH TO START?

In response, the user types in a number (which is stored in variable C).

Thus far, all of the information sought has been of a general nature. From line 54 through line 87, however, the questions become specific to individual checks. In this portion of the program, the computer asks for the name and dollar amount to be entered on each successive check. The dialogue goes like this:

FOR EACH CHECK, PLEASE PROVIDE THE FOLLOWING
INFORMATION. (EXAMPLES OF DOLLAR AMOUNT: $23402.50
THE MAXIMUM VALUE IS $999999.99)

CHECK NUMBER 101
LAST NAME?MURPHY
FIRST NAME?SAMUEL P.
DOLLAR AMOUNT?$12.95

For clarity, the user's responses have been underlined. Notice that the user in this situation has indicated that the computer should begin the sequence of checks with number 101. Hence, the computer has asked for the first and last names of the payee for check number 101 (which are stored in F$(I) and L$(I), respectively, as I is varied from 1 to N), along with the dollar amount to be paid (which is stored in A$(I)). After the dollar amount has been stored as a sequence of characters (digits), the computer goes to subroutine 300 (line 71) to examine it for errors. First, it strips off the dollar sign, which should be the first character, and checks to see whether the number is actually less than the designated maximum of 999,999.99 and whether or not a decimal point is present. If no decimal point is found, the computer assumes an even dollar amount.

The dialogue shown above is repeated until all the information for each of the N checks has been supplied. At the end of the FOR-NEXT loop in lines 60–80, the data for the I'th check have been stored as items F$(I), L$(i), and A$(I), respectively. The next step is to print each check. This is accomplished by the statements in lines 90–224 of the program, in which another FOR-NEXT loop is executed a total of N times. Inside this loop are the statements necessary to produce each check in the format indicated by the sample output shown on the following pages. Lines 99–126 concern the printing of the data, check number, and payee's name. Beginning with line 170, the program is concerned with scanning the dollar amount of each check to determine the "amount-in-words" that must appear on the face of the check. It is this part of the program that is relatively tricky. Let's see why.

Recall that the dollar amount of a check always appears in words as well as in numeric form. Hence, a check in the amount of $1,597.65 also shows the words "ONE THOUSAND FIVE HUNDRED NINETY-SEVEN AND 65/100 DOLLARS" on its face. This avoids possible confusion as to the sum involved. Since the usefulness of the check-writing program lies in the manual effort it eliminates, it is desirable for the program to generate the appropriate words automatically instead of requiring the user to supply them. Hence, the program contains statements designed to scan the dollar amount stored in A$(I) and to print the appropriate words.

How does the program do this? First, it instructs the computer to remove the cents portion of A$(I) (i.e., all characters to the right of the decimal point, if one is present) and then to divide the remaining digits into two groups of up to three characters each. The first group corresponds to thousands of dollars, while the second represents dollars. Hence, if the dollar amount in A$(I) were 223457.02, the first group of three characters would equal "223" (thousands of dollars), and the second group would equal "457" (dollars). (Note that there should be no embedded commas in the string.) On the other hand, if the dollar amount were $12.95, the first group (thousands) would be empty, and the second group would equal the two characters "12." Once this parsing of characters has been accomplished, the computer is instructed to go to subroutine 500, which prints out the words corresponding to each group of characters. The procedure here is best illustrated by an example.

Suppose the first check to be printed has a dollar amount equal to $1225.02, which is stored in A$(I). The first task is to extract the integer portion, which leaves the string "1225." (Recall that the dollar sign has already been stripped off.) Then the computer creates the first group of characters, representing thousands, and thus stores the character "1" in X$.

```
WHAT IS THE CURRENT DATE
(EXAMPLE: DECEMBER 12 1978)
?APRIL 30 1978
WHAT IS THE NAME OF YOUR COMPANY ? ACME PRODUCTS
HOW MANY CHECKS DO YOU WISH TO PRINT ? 4
WITH WHAT CHECK NUMBER DO YOU WISH TO START ?1001
FOR EACH CHECK, PLEASE PROVIDE THE FOLLOWING
INFORMATION: (EXAMPLE OF DOLLAR AMOUNT: $23402.50
THE MAXIMUM VALUE IS $999999.99)

CHECK NUMBER  1001
LAST NAME ?BAGLEY
FIRST NAME ? WARREN
DOLLAR AMOUNT ?$33.50


CHECK NUMBER  1002
LAST NAME ?BUNCZAK
FIRST NAME ? WALTER P.
DOLLAR AMOUNT ?$9999.95


CHECK NUMBER  1003
LAST NAME ?MILLER
FIRST NAME ? JANE ANN
DOLLAR AMOUNT ?$3008.85


CHECK NUMBER  1004
LAST NAME ?ROBERTS
FIRST NAME ? RUBY R.
DOLLAR AMOUNT ?$2000.00
```

```
-------------------------------------------------------------------

CHECK NUMBER  1001                            APRIL 30 1978

PAY TO THE ORDER OF.....WARREN BAGLEY.....................  $33.50

       THIRTY-THREE AND 50/100 DOLLARS

                   SIGNED--
                         A C M E   P R O D U C T S
-------------------------------------------------------------------

CHECK NUMBER  1002                            APRIL 30 1978

PAY TO THE ORDER OF.....WALTER P. BUNCZAK.................  $9999.95

        NINE THOUSAND NINE HUNDRED NINETY-NINE AND 95/100 DOLLARS

                   SIGNED--
                         A C M E   P R O D U C T S
-------------------------------------------------------------------

CHECK NUMBER  1003                            APRIL 30 1978

PAY TO THE ORDER OF.....JANE ANN MILLER...................  $3008.85

       THREE THOUSAND-EIGHT AND 85/100 DOLLARS

                   SIGNED--
                         A C M E   P R O D U C T S
-------------------------------------------------------------------

CHECK NUMBER  1004                            APRIL 30 1978

PAY TO THE ORDER OF.....RUBY R. ROBERTS..................  $2000.00

       TWO THOUSAND AND 00/100 DOLLARS

                   SIGNED--
                         A C M E   P R O D U C T S
-------------------------------------------------------------------
```

Upon reaching subroutine 500, the computer employs two string lists for printing the appropriate words. (These lists were initialized in lines 27–35.) The first is list S\$, which has 19 items. The first item equals the explicit string "ONE", the second item equals "TWO", and so on, up to item 19, which equals "NINETEEN". The second list, R\$, contains only eight items, corresponding to the words "TWENTY", "THIRTY", "FORTY", etc., through "NINETY". To print out the correct items from each list, the computer first finds the numeric value of the first character in X\$, which in this case is the number 1, and stores it in variable J. It also computes the value of the entire contents of X\$, which again equals 1, and stores that quantity in variable K. If K is found equal to zero (line 520), there is nothing to print, and the computer returns to the main program. If K is not equal to zero, however, the computer goes to line 550 where the contents of S\$(J) are printed (followed by a semicolon in the PRINT statement). This produces the word:

ONE

on the face of the check. The computer then returns to the main program where, since it is still concerned with the first group of three characters representing thousands of dollars, the word "THOUSAND" is printed next (again followed by a semicolon in the PRINT statement).

The program now extracts the second group of characters in A$(I), which equals "225". This is done in lines 180–185. X$ thus contains the string "225" when the computer goes to subroutine 500 for the second time. At this point, you might wish to "play computer" with this subroutine. You will see that the words printed out by applying the procedure we went through above will be:

TWO HUNDRED TWENTY-FIVE

Further, they will appear on the same line as the previous ones. When the computer returns from subroutine 500 this time, it will print the cents portion of the amount (lines 200–216). To do this it prints the digits to the right of the decimal point; or, if there is no decimal point, it prints the explicit string "00". The appropriate digits are printed in this case as:

AND 02/100 DOLLARS

And that is the end of the printing of the amount. The remaining program statements (lines 217–234) print the company name and other items at the bottom of the check.

Problems

1. In a certain state, driver's license numbers consist of 12 characters. The first five characters are the first five letters of the individual's last name. (In the event of a last name shorter than five characters, the remaining characters are filled in with randomly chosen letters.) The next two characters are the initials of the individual's first and middle names, respectively. These characters are followed by three digits, chosen randomly, and two letters, also chosen randomly.

   Write a computer program that a clerk in the Division of Driver Licensing of this state might use in assigning license numbers to new applicants. Your program should request the necessary information from the clerk, and then print the license number in the following format:

   FO-TH-EN-L943RW

   if the person's name is NORRIS LYLE FOTHERGILL, for instance.

2. Write a computer program that produces cryptograms of the sort one finds in puzzle books. Suppose someone supplies your program with a piece of

text that is stored word by word in a string list. Have the program "scramble" this text by replacing each letter of the alphabet with a different, randomly chosen letter. (If you substitute "X" for "A" in the text, don't use "X" for replacing any other letter.) Print out the scrambled text.

CHAPTER 11

Matrix Commands

The commands discussed in this chapter are particularly interesting to mathematicians; in fact, most of these commands were developed especially for them. Don't let this frighten you. Although the terminology may seem strange (mathematicians refer to tables as *matrices* and to lists as *vectors*), the tools of mathematics often have very practical applications. Matrix commands are no exception; you need not be aware of all their mathematical aspects in order to use them. And you will find that they can save you considerable programming effort.

A matrix is simply a table; therefore, all the rules for tables discussed in chapter 7 apply here. We will only develop some shortcuts for using tables; everything you can do with matrix commands can be done with the tools of chapter 7.

Initializing Matrices

The MAT (for matrix) READ command provides a shortcut way to read in a matrix. Simply say:

MAT READ X

This causes matrix X to be filled with data values, row by row. Suppose your DATA statements are:

```
900    DATA 12, 34.5, 27
901    DATA 17, 87.2, 49
902    DATA 91, 45.3, 50
```

Then, if you have said:

DIM X(3,3)

matrix X will be filled as follows:

```
 12        34.5        27
 17        87.2        49
 91        45.3        50
```

The computer fills each row, one at a time. If you want X to be filled this way:

```
 12        17        91
 34.5      87.2      45.3
 27        49        50
```

```
900     DATA 12, 17, 91
901     DATA 34.5, 87.2, 45.3
902     DATA 27, 49, 50
```

You may read more than one matrix at a time; merely separate them by commas:

MAT READ X, Y, Z

Matrix X will be read in its entirety, row by row; then matrix Y, row by row; and finally, matrix Z, row by row.

MAT INPUT works in essentially the same way, except that the numbers are obtained from the program user (and not from data statements):

MAT INPUT A
MAT INPUT A, B, C

The numbers should be input in the order that would be appropriate for DATA statements, had you used a MAT READ instead.

These commands can save you considerable effort. For example, suppose you have dimensioned table X (in a DIM statement) to have ten rows and twenty columns. Then the statement:

10   MAT READ X

is equivalent to:

```
10    FOR I = 1 TO 10
12      FOR J = 1 TO 20
14        READ X(I,J)
16      NEXT J
18    NEXT I
```

And:

10   MAT INPUT X

is equivalent to the same set of statements with line 14 replaced by:

14   INPUT X(I,J)

There are other shortcut ways to initialize matrices. If you want matrix R to contain zeros, simply say:

MAT R = ZER

If R has five rows and seven columns, it will be initialized to a 5-by-7 matrix containing zeros in every position. Or you may wish to initialize it to contain all ones. In that case say:

MAT R = CON

It will now be a 5-by-7 matrix containing ones in every position.

Finally, you may want to create what mathematicians call an *identity matrix*. This is simply a matrix having zeros everywhere except on the diagonal extending from the upper left corner to the lower right corner, where it has ones. A 3-by-3 identity matrix looks like this:

$$\begin{matrix} 1 & 0 & 0 \\ 0 & 1 & 0 \\ 0 & 0 & 1 \end{matrix}$$

A moment's reflection should convince you that only square matrices (those having the same number of rows as columns) can be initialized as identity matrices — merely because only square ones have a diagonal that starts in the upper left and ends in the lower right corner. If you don't believe it, try making an identity matrix out of a 3-row, 5-column matrix.

At any rate, an identity matrix may be created by saying:

MAT W = IDN

provided W is square.

In many systems MAT READ, MAT INPUT, MAT ZER, and MAT CON may be used to initialize lists (mathematicians call them *column vectors*). If you have a DIM statement that says:

DIM X(10), Y(45), Z(7)

it is perfectly acceptable to include these statements in your program:

```
10    MAT READ X
20    MAT Z = CON
30    MAT Y = ZER
```

However, a word of caution is in order. Some matrix commands may not work on lists—an error message may be generated. These situations can arise in some systems when you attempt to perform certain arithmetic computations (described in the next two sections). Thus if you plan to use matrix commands on a *list* of items, it is best to define the list as a matrix with one column:

DIM X(10, 1)

Then if you wish to fill it with data items, write your data statements exactly as you did in chapter 7. The MAT READ statement will then cause X(1,1) to be filled with the first data item, X(2,1) with the second, . . . , and so on.

On some occasions you may want to create something called a *row vector*—it looks just like a list that has been written across the page instead of down. If you want X to be a row vector with ten items, dimension it as follows:

DIM X(1,10)

You will see that row vectors differ from column vectors only when it comes to performing arithmetic computations on matrices or printing them. Just be sure to use two subscripts whenever you refer to a list that has been dimensioned as a matrix with one column (or row).

Dimensioning Matrices

The DIM statement tells the computer how much space to reserve for your matrices and vectors. Thus:

DIM X(5,3), Y(7,2)

specifies that X's maximum dimensions are five rows and three columns, while Y's are seven rows and two columns.[1] So long as you don't exceed these dimensions, you may redefine the size of both X and Y in your program. Suppose

1. In systems that allow zero subscripts (i.e., row zero and column zero), the maximum dimensions of X would be $(5 + 1)$ rows and $(3 + 1)$ columns, or six rows and four columns. However, in most systems, MAT commands ignore row zero and column zero. If you wish to use them, you should do so explicitly with FOR-NEXT loops.

you wish to read data into four rows and two columns of X. You may do so by writing the MAT READ command as:

MAT READ X(4,2)

The computer will then read eight data values and store them in rows 1 through 4 and in columns 1 and 2 of X. The *actual* dimensions of X will then be 4-by-2, although the computer has actually reserved room for five rows and three columns. (fifteen items). In fact, in many systems you may also say:

MAT READ X(6,2)

because only twelve items will be required. In such systems the original row and column dimensions in the DIM statement may be exceeded as long as the *total* number of items is less than the number you have reserved.

You may also specify a matrix's actual dimensions in the MAT INPUT, MAT ZER, and MAT CON statements:

MAT Q = ZER(6,3)
MAT P = CON(10,12)
MAT INPUT Z(4,6), A(2,3)

In the first case, eighteen items of Q would be initialized to zero; in the second, 120 items of P would be initialized to ones; and in the third, twenty-four values would be read into Z, followed by six values read into B.

The actual dimensions of matrices used in matrix commands must be specified somewhere in your program. If you do not do this with one of the four commands above, the computer will use your DIM statements to determine actual dimensions. And each matrix must be dimensioned explicitly. Of course, if you do not plan to use matrix commands at all, you need dimension a matrix only if its size is greater than 10-by-10 (as indicated in chapter 7).

Matrix Operations

Arithmetic may be performed on matrices. You can add two matrices by saying:

MAT C = A + B

In this case, A, B and C must have the same actual dimensions. If they do, each element in B is added to the corresponding element in A, and the result is stored in the corresponding position in C. If A is a 3-by-3 matrix containing:

3	6	2
4	1	5
9	8	7

and B is a 3-by-3 matrix containing:

2	4	7
5	3	1
2	5	3

then C will contain:

5	10	9
9	4	6
11	13	10

One matrix may be subtracted from another:

$$\text{MAT C} = A - B$$

Again, all three must have the same actual dimensions. Each element in B will be subtracted from the corresponding element in A, and the result will be stored in the corresponding position in C.

Matrices may be multiplied:

$$\text{MAT C} = A * B$$

For this operation to work the number of columns in A must equal the number of rows in B. If earlier you had said:

$$\text{MAT READ } A(4,3), B(3,7)$$

the multiplication of A times B would be appropriate. The result, C, would be a matrix having four rows (as does A) and seven columns (as does B). In every case where matrix multiplication is possible, the resulting matrix will have the same number of rows as the first matrix multiplied, and the same number of columns as the second. To avoid problems, you should make sure that C's actual dimensions have been specified appropriately.

Matrix multiplication has many practical applications. Suppose your company has three salespersons and makes five products. Monthly sales can be recorded in a 3-by-5 matrix (S):

12	17	13	7	2
9	20	15	2	8
4	7	12	14	5

Each row in S represents a salesperson; each column a product. Hence, salesperson 2 sold nine units of product 1, twenty units of product 2, and so on.

The prices of the products can be recorded in a 5-by-1 matrix P:

$$5$$
$$3$$
$$7$$
$$2$$
$$4$$

Do you want to know the total dollar sales for each salesperson? Here is a program to calculate those figures:

```
10    DIM T(3,1)
20    MAT READ S(3,5), P(5,1)
30    MAT T = S * P
40    FOR I = 1 TO 3
50      PRINT "DOLLAR SALES FOR SALESPERSON"; I; "WERE"; T(I,1)
60    NEXT I
70    STOP
```

And the data you'll need:

```
100    DATA 12,17,13,7,2
101    DATA 9,20,15,2,8
102    DATA 4,7,12,14,5
104    DATA 5,3,7,2,4
105    END
```

This is the output:

```
DOLLAR SALES FOR SALESPERSON 1  WERE  224
DOLLAR SALES FOR SALESPERSON 2  WERE  246
DOLLAR SALES FOR SALESPERSON 3  WERE  173
```

The first item (224) in the 3-by-1 matrix T equals the sum:

$$(12 * 5) + (17 * 3) + (13 * 7) + (7 * 2) + (2 * 4)$$

The general rule is this. If $T = S * P$, the element in the i'th row and k'th column of T is always computed in the following way:

$$T(I,K) = \sum_{J=1}^{M} S(I,J) * P(J,K)$$

where M is the number of columns in S and the number of rows in P. Try this formula to verify that $T(2,1)$ and $T(3,1)$ are 246 and 173, respectively.

It is also possible to multiply a matrix by a single number or by the value of any arithmetic expression. Just enclose the expression in parentheses and place it in front of the matrix:

$$\text{MAT } F = (N * (K + 2)) * G$$
$$\text{MAT } H = (.5) * I$$

The result is the original matrix with each element multiplied by the value of the arithmetic expression. Obviously, both matrices must have the same actual dimensions. If the number by which you are multiplying is 1, you may write:

$$\text{MAT } M = N$$

instead of:

$$\text{MAT } M = (1) * N$$

Either way, matrix M would end up as an exact copy of matrix N.

Only one arithmetic operation may be performed in a single MAT command. It is illegal to write:

$$\text{MAT } C = A * B - D$$

But you can do the job in stages:

$$\text{MAT } E = A * B$$
$$\text{MAT } C = E - D$$

The same matrix may appear on both sides of the equal sign in statements involving addition, subtraction, or multiplication by a constant, but not in statements involving matrix multiplication. There is a reason for this rule. Think about the following illegal command:

$$\text{MAT } C = A * C$$

As each new element is computed and stored in C, one of the original values still needed for subsequent computations is being destroyed! Hardly a satisfactory situation.

Two concluding observations should be made concerning the above matrix operations. First, some systems allow you to redimension the matrix referenced on the left of the equal sign in these statements. Thus, if the matrix to be altered does not have the proper dimensions for the operation being performed, you can do something about it on the spot. For instance, suppose somewhere in your program you had previously said:

$$\text{DIM } M(3,5), A(2,2), C(2,2)$$

and now you wish to add C to A and store the result in M. Just say:

$$\text{MAT } M(2,2) = A + C$$

or, alternatively, if you wish to multiply A and C and place the product in M, you can say:

$$MAT\ M(2,2) = A * C$$

Second, if you do redimension a matrix using any of these matrix operation statements, do not refer to the same matrix on both sides of the equal sign, as in MAT A(10,3) = A * R. Most computers will not accept such statements.

Additional Matrix Operations

Two other operations involving matrices can be extremely useful. The first helps solve sets of simultaneous linear equations. Suppose you wish to find values for X and Y that satisfy the following equations:

$$2X + Y = 9$$
$$4X + 3Y = 15$$

Let matrix A contain the coefficients on the left-hand sides of the equations. It will be a 2-by-2 matrix containing:

$$2 \quad\quad 1$$
$$4 \quad\quad 3$$

Next, let B equal a 2-by-1 matrix containing the constants on the right-hand sides of the equations:

$$9$$
$$15$$

Finally, let V be a 2-by-1 matrix containing the unknown values of X and Y. How can we find these values? By using the matrix *inversion* command:

$$MAT\ C = INV(A)$$

V can be determined directly from C. It is given by:

$$MAT\ V = C * B$$

After execution of this statement, V(1,1) will contain the value of variable X, and V(2,1) will contain the value of Y.

We shall not go into all the details of matrix inversion. If you wish to know more about it, you should consult any standard college algebra text. However, it should be pointed out that the matrix inverted (in this case, A) must be square. This is equivalent to the familiar requirement that there be as many variables as there are equations. If there are more equations than variables, one equation may be redundant. For example:

$$2X + \ Y = \ 9$$
$$4X + 3Y = 15$$
$$8X + 6Y = 30$$

(Here the last equation can be derived from the second by multiplying the latter by 2.) Alternatively, some of the equations may be inconsistent. For example:

$$2X + \ Y = \ 9$$
$$4X + 3Y = 15$$
$$4X + 3Y = 20$$

As you can see, there are no solutions to this set of equations. If, on the other hand, there are fewer equations than variables, several values of X and Y may satisfy the equations. Here is an example having an infinite number of solutions:

$$2X + \ Y = \ 9$$

Even though a matrix is square, it may not have an inverse. This is reasonable enough—some systems of linear equations simply have no solution. It is quite possible, for example, to write a set of N equations having N unknowns and at least one inconsistency. A matrix that has no inverse is termed *singular*; not surprisingly, one that does have an inverse is called *nonsingular*. In most systems the computer will print an error message and quit if you try to invert a singular matrix. In some, however, you can find out whether a matrix is singular after attempting to invert it. If the *determinant* is set to zero after inversion, the matrix was singular.[2] You might thus say:

```
10    MAT C = INV(A)
20    LET D = DET
30    IF D = 0 THEN 100
```

DET is a special function; it assumes the value of the determinant of the last matrix inverted.[3]

The inverse of a matrix is the same size as the matrix itself. In the example above if A is a 4-by-4 matrix, the dimensions of C must also be 4-by-4.

2. The determinant is a numeric value computed from the elements of the matrix. For present purposes, it suffices to know that the determinant of a singular matrix will equal zero. As a practical matter, the inverse is likely to be unreliable if the determinant differs only slightly from zero.

3. In some systems, you must specify when using DET which matrix you are referencing. Hence, if you wished to find the determinant of A, you would say in line 20 above:

```
20    LET D = DET(A)
```

Another matrix operation is *transposition*. Matrix B is said to be the transpose of A if it is a carbon copy of A with the rows and columns of the latter interchanged. Thus

2	4	7
3	5	9

is the transpose of:

2	3
4	5
7	9

If the original matrix has two rows and three columns, the transpose will have three rows and two columns. Since row 1 of the first matrix becomes column 1 of the second, and row 2 of the first becomes column 2 of the second, and so on, you could accomplish a transposition with this program segment:

```
60     FOR I = 1 TO 3
65        FOR J = 1 TO 5
70           LET B(J,I) = A(I,J)
75        NEXT J
80     NEXT I
```

But it is much easier simply to say:

$$MAT\ B = TRN(A)$$

Just be sure that the number of rows in B equals the number of columns in A, and the number of columns in B equals the number of rows in A.

Printing Matrices

The command:

$$MAT\ PRINT\ X$$

will cause the values in matrix X to be printed on per zone across the output sheet. The items will be printed row by row—first the items in row 1, then row 2, and so on. Should any row have more than the number of items allowed per line (five on most systems), additional lines will be required. And when the end of a row is reached, a new line will be started. To illustrate, if X equals:

10	47.3	16	7	0.5	32
37	53	98.8	2	0.9	32.15

the output would be:

10	47.3	16	7	0.5
32				
37	53	98.8	2	0.9
32.15				

If X were a 3-row, 1-column vector containing:

$$10$$
$$47.3$$
$$16$$

the output would be:

$$10$$
$$47.3$$
$$16$$

Several matrices may be printed in one command:

MAT PRINT X, Y, Z,

In many systems, a comma following a matrix name indicates that each row is to be printed with one item per zone across the output sheet. Thus, the dangling comma in this command is not an ordinary dangling comma. It simply tells the computer to print the items in each row of Z one per zone. If no comma appears after the last matrix indicated, it will be assumed.

If you want the items more closely spaced on the output sheet, you may write:

MAT PRINT X;

or:

MAT PRINT X;Y;Z;

These statements will cause the items in each row to be printed with only one space between them across the page, but each row will begin on a new line.

Semicolons and commas may be mixed:

MAT PRINT X, Y; Z,

In each case the punctuation *after* the matrix name determines its spacing on the page.

In some systems, you may use MAT PRINT to print only a portion of a matrix. Suppose, for instance, that you have the following dimension statement in your program.

DIM C(100,5)

and you wish to print out the contents of only the first 10 rows of C. Simply say:

MAT PRINT C(10,5),

This statement would result in fifty values being output with one value per print zone. When dimensions are indicated this way in a MAT PRINT statement, the matrix is not redimensioned as is the case with other MAT commands in which dimensions are indicated. In this case, the subscripts just tell the computer the maximum number of values to print.

Here is a program to solve our set of simultaneous linear equations and MAT PRINT the results:

```
10      DIM A(2,2),B(2,1),C(2,2),X(2,1)
15      REM -- READ IN  A AND B
20      MAT   READ A,B
25      PRINT "HERE ARE MATRICES A AND B:"
28      MAT   PRINT A,B,
30      REM -- FIND SOLUTION
32      MAT C=INV(A)
34      PRINT
36      PRINT "HERE IS THE INVERSE OF A:"
38      MAT   PRINT C
40      MAT X = C * B
42      PRINT
44      PRINT "AND HERE IS THE SOLUTION FOR X AND Y:"
46      MAT   PRINT X
200     DATA 2,1
210     DATA 4,3
220     DATA 9,15
300     END
```

The output, as you might expect, is:

```
HERE ARE MATRICES A AND B:
 2               1

 4               3

 9

 15


HERE IS THE INVERSE OF A:
 1.5            -.5

-2               1


AND HERE IS THE SOLUTION FOR X AND Y:
 6

-3
```

An Application

To indicate that matrix operations are by no means limited to mathematical applications, we revised the security analysis program of chapter 7, using some matrix commands. The result was a much simpler program. Here it is:

```
10    REM -- SECURITY ANALYSIS PROGRAM
11    REM
12    REM -- SET UP DIMENSIONS
13    LET N = 10
14    LET M = 6
15    DIM S[10,6],T[10,1],U[1,6]
20    REM -- READ IN SECURITY DATA
21    MAT   READ S[N,M]
22    PRINT "SECURITY DATA:"
23    PRINT
24    MAT   PRINT S;
26    PRINT
30    REM -- PRINT HEADINGS
35    PRINT "SECURITY","AVERAGE PRICE","STD DEVIATION"
37    PRINT
40    REM -- FIND AVERAGE PRICE, STD DEVIATION
42    MAT C = CON[M,1]
44    MAT T = S * C
45    MAT T = (1/M) * T
47    FOR I = 1 TO N
48    LET T2 = 0
50    FOR J = 1 TO M
52    LET T2 = T2 + ((S[I,J]-T[I,1])^2)
54    NEXT J
55    LET D = (T2/M)^.5
56    PRINT I,.01 * INT((T[I,1]*100+.5),.01 * INT((D*100)+.5)
58    NEXT I
59    PRINT
60    REM -- PRINT HEADINGS
62    PRINT "MONTH","AVG--ALL STOCKS"
64    PRINT
70    REM -- NOW FIND MONTHLY AVERAGES
72    MAT C = CON[1,N]
74    MAT U = C * S
76    MAT U = (1/N)*U
78    FOR J = 1 TO M
79    PRINT J,.01 * INT((U[1,J]*100+.5)
80    NEXT J
90    STOP
```

To test the program, we made up this set of data:

```
800    DATA 24.5,30,29,25,27.875,32.125,51.75
810    DATA 50,51.25,52.375,51.625,51.625,52.5
820    DATA 37.375,36.875,35,35.125,35.875,35
830    DATA 86.25,88.125,88,87.625,87.5,88.625
840    DATA 22.5,22.5,22.125,22.625,22,23.125
850    DATA 100.24,102.5,103,104.5,103.626,104.125
860    DATA 50.25,50.125,50.375,52.5,52,51.75
870    DATA 90.5,90.75,93.75,92.875,95,94.125
880    DATA 10.125,9.625,8.75,11.25,11,10.75
890    DATA 40.625,42.375,42,45.125,46,46.875
```

This new program produces the same results as the old one and prints the security data as well. We did, however, round the average prices, standard deviations, and monthly averages to make the output easier to read. This is the output, using the above data for ten stocks over a six-month period:

```
SECURITY DATA:

24.5          30    29.25      27.875      32.125      31.75

50     51.25         52.375     51.625      51.625      52.5

37.375    36.875    35    35.125      35.875      35

86.25     88.125    88    87.625      87.5        88.625

22.5      22.5      22.125     22.675      22      23.125

100.24    102.5     103    104.5       103.626     104.125

50.25     50.125    50.375     52.5        52      51.75

90.5      90.75     93.75      92.875      95      94.125

10.125    9.675     8.75       11.25       11      10.75

40.675    42.375    42    45.125      46      46.875

SECURITY          AVERAGE PRICE    STD DEVIATION

1                 29.25            2.57
2                 51.56            .83
3                 35.88            .94
4                 87.69            .74
5                 22.49            .37
6                 103              1.4
7                 51.17            .95
8                 92.83            1.68
9                 10.26            .86
10                43.84            2.28

MONTH          AVG--ALL STOCKS

1                 51.24
2                 52.42
3                 52.46
4                 53.12
5                 53.68
6                 53.86
```

Problems

1. What, if anything, is wrong with this program segment?

```
10    DIM X(4,5)
12    MAT READ X(2,3)
13    MAT Y = ZER(3,2)
14    MAT Y = TRN(X)
```

```
15    MAT PRINT X;Y;
20    MAT READ X(4,4)
22    MAT Y = IDN(4,4)
23    MAT Z = ZER(4,4)
25    MAT Z = X * Y
26    MAT PRINT X;Y;Z,
30    STOP
```

```
10    MAT READ R(3,4)
20    MAT R=TRN(R)
```

3. Write a program segment that creates a 4-by-4 square matrix having ones everywhere, except on the diagonal extending from the upper-left corner to the lower-right corner. Put zeros along this diagonal.

4. Write a program segment to solve this set of equations. Include data statements and print results.

$$4X + Y + Z = -17$$
$$X + 2Y + Z = -5$$
$$2X + 7Y - Z = 53$$

Answers

1. Nothing. It is legal to redefine the *actual* dimensions of a matrix as often as desired, so long as these new dimensions don't exceed those specified in the DIM statement (or 10-by-10 if no DIM statement is given).

2. No. The transposed matrix will not have the right dimensions to be stored back in R. To avoid the problem, say:

$$\text{DIM S(4,3)}$$
$$\text{MAT S = TRN(R)}$$

3. This is not as difficult as you might think. C is the matrix we want:

```
100    MAT A=CON(4,4)
105    MAT B=IDN(4,4)
110    MAT C=A-B
```

4. Whenever you attempt to solve a set of simultaneous linear equations, make sure the equations are in the proper form. The coefficients for each variable must represent a single column, and all the constants must be on one side of the equal signs. Since the equations given here are already in

the appropriate form, we can set up the data for the coefficient matrix (A) and the constant matrix (B) directly:

```
100    REM -- DATA FOR MATRIX A
101    DATA 4, 1, 1
102    DATA 1, 2, 1
103    DATA 2, 7, -1
105    REM -- DATA FOR MATRIX B
106    DATA -17, -5, 53
110    END
```

```
10     DIM A(3,3), B(3,1), C(3,3), V(3,1)
15     REM -- READ A AND B
16     MAT READ A, B
20     MAT C = INV(A)
22     MAT V = C * B
24     PRINT "HERE IS THE SOLUTION FOR X, Y, Z:"
25     MAT PRINT V
30     STOP
```

Only the dimension statement (and data, of course) need be changed to solve any other legal set of equations.

CHAPTER 12

Additional Features

In recent years, the BASIC language has become immensely popular. Because of this, it has been implemented on an extensive variety of computer systems, ranging in size from the largest-scale scientific machines to the smallest of microcomputers. One of the inevitable consequences of such proliferation is nonstandardization of the language's features from one computer to the next.

This chapter discusses some of the features that are not as widely available or as standardized across BASIC systems as one might like. In spite of this, many of these features are just as useful as those discussed in earlier chapters. You might even find some of them indispensable for particular applications.

Happily, some features described in this chapter are available on many systems. They include the modified LET statement, the computed GOSUB, and multiple-argument user-defined functions. But be forewarned about the features discussed here in general. Many—especially appended clauses, expanded IF statements, and data files—just haven't been implemented on different computers in a consistent fashion. The best defense we know in such instances is consultation with the reference manual supplied by the manufacturer of your computer. Do this *before* you try anything fancy.

Modified LET Statements

The conventional LET statement has the form:

LET *variable* = *expression*

The expression on the right-hand side of the equal sign is evaluated; then the result is assigned to the variable named on the left-hand side.

Thus far we have insisted that every line number be followed by some sort of identification of the type of statement to follow. The computer then knows immediately whether it is to PRINT, GO TO, RETURN, and so on, or if it is about to encounter a REMark, DIMension statement, or the like. The command LET indicates that an *assignment statement* is to follow. And it makes perfectly clear to the computer, the programmer, and anyone reading the program exactly what is going to happen.

But one can easily tire of writing LET; and assignment statements are used more frequently than any other type. For this reason almost all systems allow you to omit it. Instead of:

$$10 \quad \text{LET } X = 3$$

you may, if you wish, write:

$$10 \quad X = 3$$

But beware — this may make your program harder for others to understand. And it could even confuse you.

Sometime you may want to assign the same value to a number of variables. For example:

```
10    LET S1 = 0
12    LET S2 = 0
14    LET S3 = 0
16    LET S4 = 0
```

Most systems provide a shorthand method for accomplishing this. The most common involves repeated use of the equal sign:

$$10 \quad \text{LET } S1 = S2 = S3 = S4 = 0$$

The expression on the right-hand side is evaluated; then the result is assigned to the rightmost variable (here, S4); then it is assigned to the next variable (here, S3); and so on.

Some systems use a slightly different construction:

$$10 \quad \text{LET } S1, S2, S3, S4 = 0$$

A few systems provide somewhat less help. The best possible solution to the problem may just be:

$$10 \quad \text{LET } S1 = 0, S2 = 0, S3 = 0, S4 = 0$$

Whatever the procedure, the goal is the same—to allow you to write your instructions more succinctly.

The Computed GOSUB

Remember the ON statement discussed in chapter 3? It allows you to test the value of an expression and then branch to any one of several statements, depending upon the value found.

There is one more thing you can do with the ON statement: test the value of an expression and branch to any one of several *subroutines*. This use of the ON statement is analogous to the normal use. The only difference in most systems is that you say ON . . . GOSUB . . . instead of ON . . . GO TO. . . . For instance,

ON X-Y GOSUB 400, 600, 200, 800, 90

tests the value of the expression X-Y. If it equals 1, the computer executes subroutine 400; if it equals 2, the computer executes subroutine 600, and so on. When the appropriate subroutine has been executed, the computer returns to the statement immediately following the ON . . . GOSUB.

In systems that use a different form for the computed GOSUB, you may have to say:

GOSUB X-Y ON 400, 600, 200, 800, 90

or even:

GOSUB X-Y OF 400, 600, 200, 800, 90

But no matter. These various forms do the same thing. Each allows you to provide any arithmetic expression to be evaluated (although some computers may *truncate* the resulting value to a whole number while others may *round* it). If the *resulting whole number* value equals n, the computer will go to the nth subroutine in the list. Thus, if n equals 5, the computer will execute the fifth subroutine listed.

More User-defined Functions

As we noted in chapter 8, the computer will let you define your own functions. This is particularly useful whenever there is no "canned" function that does what you have in mind. By using the DEF command, you can indicate what expression you wish to have evaluated each time you refer to a particular function. Recall that functions discussed in chapter 8 could have either zero or one argument.

In many systems, user-defined functions may legally have more than one argument, or parameter. This allows you to write somewhat more complex and versatile expressions than you can if restricted to just one argument. When defining a function of several parameters, simply separate them by commas:

```
100    DEF FNG(X,Y)      = (X + (2*Y))^3
101    DEF FNH(A,B,C,)    = (A * B * C/SQR((A^2)+(B^2)+(C^2)))
102    DEF FNW(L,M,N,P)   = (LOG(L+M+N+P)/4) + FNG(3.7,8)
```

Needless to say, you should give the function the right number of arguments when you refer to it elsewhere:

```
500    LET R7 = FNW(R,49,Q(J),A5*7)
520    LET T(K,1) = FNG(FNH(2,D,4), 35)
```

The computer will assign each value to its corresponding parameter in the DEF statement. Accordingly, line 520 specifies that the value of FNH(2,D,4) is to be assigned to parameter X of FNG(X,Y), whereas 35 is to be assigned to parameter Y.

In addition to multiple-argument functions, some systems allow you to define functions whose formulas cannot be written in a single (one-line) DEF statement. For example, you may want to define the routine that computes the factorial of a number as a function. This is one way:

```
10    DEF FNF(N)
12       LET FNF = N
14       FOR M = N-1 TO 1 STEP -1
16          LET FNF = FNF * M
18       NEXT M
20    FNEND
```

Another example of a multiple-line function is the following, which computes the greatest divisor for any positive or negative integer (whole number):

```
30    DEF FND(M)
32       FOR I9 = ABS(INT(M/2)) TO 1 STEP -1
34          IF M/I9 = INT(M/I9) THEN 38
36       NEXT I9
38       LET FND = I9
40    FNEND
```

When the computer encounters the DEF statements for FNF(N) and FND(M), it assumes they have multiple-line definitions because there is no " = " sign in either DEF statement. Therefore, it looks for "FNEND." Everything between DEF and FNEND is assumed to be part of the definition.

Notice how the value is assigned to this type of function. The function name is used as a kind of "temporary variable" inside the definition. The last value assigned to this temporary variable is used as the value of the function. This is just what you'd want to happen. When you refer to a multiple-line function in your program, the computer will execute the definition (replacing any parameters by the values you specify as arguments), then assign the function whatever value it has when the FNEND statement is reached.

All the other rules for functions apply as before. In addition to parameters, regular variables may be used inside a definition; they are *global* to the program. Thus M in FNF(N) is a global variable, and so is I9 in FND(M). But the function name and any parameters specified are local to the definition. Thus N is local to FNF(N), and M is local to FND(M). In many systems a multiple-line function may have zero, one, or more parameters.

One last point. In some systems you are allowed to define certain variables as local to a function (in addition to the parameters, which are always local). This is sometimes quite useful, especially if you want to avoid altering the values of any global variables inside the function. Thus we might make I9 local to FND(M) by replacing line 30 with:

30   DEF FND(M) I9

From that point on, the I9 used by the function will bear no relationship to the I9 used in the rest of the program.

Several variables may be defined as local with systems that have this feature. Merely place them all at the end of the DEF statement and separate them with commas:

100   DEF FNX(S,T) U7, V, R6

A Useful Function

As noted, user-defined functions can be very handy, particularly if you have a messy formula to evaluate repeatedly. To illustrate the use of multiple-argument functions, assume you wish to generate random numbers that come from a normally distributed population having an average value (mean) of zero and a standard deviation of 1. Roughly speaking, this means that if you were to divide the interval between -5 and $+5$ into many smaller intervals of equal length, generate a great many random numbers, and plot on a graph the number in each interval, you would find that this "frequency diagram" would have a "bell shape." Values close to the mean would occur more frequently than others, with about 68 percent falling in the interval between -1 and $+1$.

It is clear that RND can't be used for this purpose because the numbers it generates are uniformly distributed and are restricted to values between zero and 1. This means that values around the mean (.50) are no more likely to occur than values very close to zero or to 1. But it is possible to transform uniform random numbers into approximately normal ones. Here's a two-argument function that does it:

DEF FNR(X,Y) = SQR($-$ LOG(X))*(COS(6.283185*Y) + SIN(6.28315*Y))

FNR(X,Y) requires you to supply it with uniform random numbers; one is X, the other is Y. Hence, the program segment within which FNR(X,Y) appears might look like this:

LET X = RND
LET Y = RND
LET Z = FNR(X,Y)

If you want to know why this function happens to generate normally distributed random numbers, consult the reference in the footnote.[1]

To test FNR, 10,000 random numbers were generated, and those falling into each of eight intervals (less than or equal to -3, greater than -3 and less than or equal to -2, greater than -2 to less than or equal to -1, and so on, up to greater than $+3$) counted. The mean and standard deviations were also computed.[2] Here is the program:

---

1. See G. E. P. Box and M. E. Miller, "A Note on the Generation of Normal Deviates," *Ann. Math. Stat.* 29:610–11.
2. The standard deviation was computed with a "shortcut" formula, but the result should be the same as that obtained with the longer formula introduced in chapter 6. Statistically speaking, a slightly better estimate of the "true" population standard deviation could have been obtained with the following formula:

90   LET S = SQR(((T2) $-$ ((T1 2)/10000))/9999)

However, because our sample is so large (10,000), the difference between the two formulas should be slight.

```
10    REM -- GENERATE 10,000 RANDOM NORMALLY DISTRIBUTED NUMBERS
11    REM
20    DEF FNR(X,Y) = SQR(-LOG(X)) * (COS(6.28318*X)+SIN(6.28318*X))
30    REM -- COMPUTE THE NUMBER OF RANDOM NUMBERS FALLING INTO EIGHT
31    REM -- INTERVALS AROUND THE MEAN. ALSO COMPUTE MEAN, STD. DEV.
40    REM -- INITIALIZE COUNTERS
41    FOR J = 1 TO 8
42    LET T[J] = 0
43    NEXT J
45    LET T1 = T2 = 0
47    RANDOMIZE
50    REM -- GENERATE EACH NUMBER, ADD TO TOTALS
52    FOR I = 1 TO 10000
54    LET X = RND
55    LET Y = RND
56    LET Z = FNR(X,Y)
57    LET T1 = T1 + Z
58    LET T2 = T2 + (Z^2)
59    IF Z >= 0 THEN 75
60    GOTO (INT(-Z)+1) OF 72,70,65
63    LET T[1] = T[1] + 1
64    GOTO 86
65    LET T[2] = T[2] + 1
67    GOTO 86
70    LET T[3] = T[3] + 1
71    GOTO 86
72    LET T[4] = T[4] + 1
73    GOTO 86
75    GOTO (INT(Z)+1) OF 78,80,85
76    LET T[8] = T[8] + 1
77    GOTO 86
78    LET T[5] = T[5] + 1
79    GOTO 86
80    LET T[6] = T[6] + 1
82    GOTO 86
85    LET T[7] = T[7] + 1
86    NEXT I
87    REM -- COMPUTE STANDARD DEVIATION
90    LET S = SQR((T2/10000) - ((T1/10000)^2))
92    REM -- PRINT RESULTS
93    PRINT "THERE WERE ";T[1];TAB(22);NUMBERS LESS THAN OR EQUAL TO -3"
95    FOR J= 2 TO 7
96    PRINT "THERE WERE ";T[J];TAB(22);NUMBERS IN INTERVAL ";J-5;"TO";J-4
98    NEXT J
99    PRINT "THERE WERE ";T[8];TAB(22);"NUMBERS GREATER THAN +3"
100   PRINT
102   PRINT "THE MEAN WAS APPROXIMATELY ";.01*(INT(100*(T1/10000)+.5))
104   PRINT
106   PRINT "THE STANDARD DEVIATION WAS APPROXIMATELY ";
108   PRINT .01 * (INT((100*S)+.5))
110   END
```

And here are its results:

```
THERE WERE 11         NUMBERS LESS THAN OR EQUAL TO -3
THERE WERE 238        NUMBERS IN INTERVAL -3    TO-2
THERE WERE 1346       NUMBERS IN INTERVAL -2    TO-1
THERE WERE 3375       NUMBERS IN INTERVAL -1    TO 0
THERE WERE 3426       NUMBERS IN INTERVAL  0    TO 1
THERE WERE 1376       NUMBERS IN INTERVAL  1    TO 2
THERE WERE 211        NUMBERS IN INTERVAL  2    TO 3
THERE WERE 17         NUMBERS GREATER THAN +3

THE MEAN WAS APPROXIMATELY .02

THE STANDARD DEVIATION WAS APPROXIMATELY  .99
```

As you can see, 6,801 numbers — or 68.01 percent of the 10,000 random numbers — were within one unit of zero — that is, between − 1 and + 1. Notice, too, that the mean (0.02) and the standard deviation (0.99) are very close to zero and 1, respectively. And the distribution is reasonably symmetric; nearly as many numbers fell below zero (4,970) as above zero (5,030). These results suggest that FNR may be quite a good normal-random-number generator. Of course, more precise testing of the quality of the approximation would involve additional statistical measurement.

Expanded IF Statements

Some systems allow IF statements of the form:

| IF | *arithmetic expression* | *comparison* | *arithmetic expression* | THEN | *statement* |

or

| IF | *string expression* | *comparison* | *string expression* | THEN | *statement* |

The statement following "THEN" may usually be any legal statement except DATA, REM, FOR, or NEXT. In each case, if the condition specified is true, the computer executes the statement following THEN; otherwise, it goes to the statement after the IF command. This allows statements such as:

40   IF A = F THEN PRINT "A EQUALS F"

or any of the following:

```
50   IF Z3 > Z4 THEN GOSUB 400
75   IF W$(5) <> W$(6) THEN READ Z$(1)
80   IF (R + W) * 2 = INT(LOG(Q5)) THEN RETURN
```

A few systems even allow you to specify the action to be taken if the condition is false, as in:

50 IF D = 29 THEN GO TO 1233 ELSE RETURN

The statement after "THEN" will be executed if the condition is true; but the statement after "ELSE" will be executed if the condition is false. In this case both statements cause a transfer to some other part of the program, but this is not necessary, as the following program segment illustrates:

```
50    IF X > 0 THEN LET S = 0 ELSE LET S = 1
60    PRINT S
```

Variable S will be set to zero (if X is positive) or 1 (if X is not positive). Then its value will be printed.

Whenever an IF statement does not cause a transfer to another part of the program, the next statement in line will be executed.

Logical Expressions

Thus far we have encountered two types of expressions. *Arithmetic expressions* are combinations of constants, variables, and arithmetic operators. When such expressions are evaluated, the result is always a number. The other type of expression considered explicitly in earlier chapters was termed a *string expression*. When it is evaluated, the result is a string of characters.

There is yet another type of expression—the *logical expression*. Its distinguishing characteristic is simple enough: The value of a logical expression is either *true* or *false*.

Using the definition of a logical expression, we can describe the standard IF statement very succinctly. It is simply:

IF *logical expression*   THEN   *line number*

For we have been using logical expressions all along. Consider the statement:

IF   A > 3   THEN 200

This can be interpreted in the following way: "If the statement 'A is greater than 3' is *true*, go to line number 200; if the statement is *false*, continue."

Obviously, (A > 3) is a logical expression. Some other examples are:

$$A\$ = B\$$$
$$(A + B) > = (C/D)$$
$$X < 3.5$$

Some systems allow you to write more complex logical expressions. Particularly useful are the relations AND and OR.

For example, assume that you want to go to line 200 if A9 is between 3 and 5. Using simple logical expressions you might have to say something like this:

```
100    IF A9 <= 3 THEN 110
105    IF A9 < 5 THEN 200
110    REM -- A9 IS NOT BETWEEN 3 AND 5
```

But the job can be done with one statement, using AND:

$$100 \quad \text{IF} (A9 > 3) \quad \text{AND} (A9 < 5) \quad \text{THEN} \, 200$$

Note that everything between IF and THEN constitutes the logical expression. It is, in turn, made up from two other logical expressions. The truth or falsity of the overall expression depends, of course, on the truth or falsity of the component expressions. In fact, AND is formally defined with a *truth-table* of the following variety:

LE-1	LE-2	(LE-1 AND LE-2)
True	True	True
True	False	False
False	True	False
False	False	False

LE-1 stands for any logical expression; LE-2 stands for any other logical expression. The table simply indicates that the conjunction of two logical expressions is true only if both components are true. This accords with everyday usage of the term AND.

What if you would like to transfer to line 200 if A9 is less than 3 or greater than 5? Nothing to it, if your system allows the OR relation:

$$100 \quad \text{IF} (A9 < 3) \quad \text{OR} \quad (A9 > 5) \quad \text{THEN} \, 200$$

The meaning of the term OR can also be shown with a truth-table:

LE-1	LE-2	(LE-1 OR LE-2)
True	True	True
True	False	True
False	True	True
False	False	False

In other words, (LE-1 OR LE-2) is true if either one of the two components is true (or if both are true). This accords with most usages of the word OR and with the meaning of the legal term "and/or."

Some systems allow you to get very fancy indeed. But be certain to use parentheses liberally to avoid ambiguity. For example:

$$\text{IF} \; ((A9 > 4) \; \text{AND} (B3 = 5)) \; \text{OR} \; ((B3 < A9) \; \text{AND} \; (X = .2)) \; \text{THEN} \; 200$$

In many cases you may be allowed to do even more than this with logical expressions. But the ability to use AND and OR in an IF statement is likely to prove the most valuable extension to the concept of a logical expression for most applications.

Appended Clauses

Some systems allow you to append one or more clauses to certain state-ments; the clause or clauses specify the conditions under which the statement is to be executed. A simple (though hardly exciting) illustration is provided by the appended IF clause. For example:

$$100 \quad \text{LET } X = 3 \quad \text{IF } X < 0$$

The statement "LET $X = 3$" will be executed if the condition is met (i.e., if X is less than zero). Otherwise the statement will not be executed at all, and the program will pass to the next statement in line.

Obviously, an appended IF clause has the same effect as the IF . . . THEN construction. Thus one might write:

$$100 \quad \text{IF } X < 0 \quad \text{THEN LET } X = 3$$

Some of the other clauses that may be appended are more novel. For exam-ple, consider the following statement:

$$100 \quad \text{LET } X = X - 5 \quad \text{WHILE } X > = 5$$

This instructs the computer to execute the statement "LET $X = X - 5$" over and over again as long as X remains above 5. This will eventually set X equal to the remainder that would have been obtained had the original value been divided by 5.

The UNLESS clause indicates that a statement is to be executed unless the specified condition is met. For example:

$$10 \quad \text{PRINT "HI THERE" UNLESS N\$ = "MURPHY"}$$

Perhaps the most useful type of appended clause is FOR. Let's say that you want to read fifty values into list X. Ordinarily, this would require three state-ments.

```
15    FOR I = 1 TO 50
17      READ X(I)
19    NEXT I
```

But it can all be accomplished with one statement, using an appended FOR clause:

$$15 \quad \text{READ } X(I) \quad \text{FOR } I = 1 \text{ TO } 50$$

This is simply a shorthand method for writing FOR-NEXT loops; but it is convenient, nonetheless.

You may be able to save even more effort by using two or more appended clauses. The general rule is this: The rightmost clause is considered first, then the next one, and so on. For example, assume that you want to print the entries of table T. The conventional way to do it might look like this:

```
10   FOR I = 1 TO M
12      FOR J = 1 TO N
14         PRINT T(I,J)
16      NEXT J
18   NEXT I
```

But with appended FOR clauses the five lines could be replaced by one:

10   PRINT T(I,J)   FOR J = 1 TO N   FOR I = 1 TO M

Appended clauses are helpful, though hardly essential. If your system offers them, use them — but with care.

Data Files

Most systems provide built-in file storage. The information is often stored on magnetic disks that rotate constantly at a rather high speed. But you need not concern yourself with such details. Just think of a *file* as another data list of numbers and/or strings.

Unfortunately, computer filing systems are no more standardized than traditional filing systems. Every one is a little different. Some allow only the simplest kinds of storage and retrieval; others provide all sorts of options.

This is not the place for an extended discussion of various alternatives. Instead, we will merely introduce a few fundamental ideas, using constructs from a representative system. Although other systems vary in detail, the general principles are the same.

Because any given user can have many files, each file must be given a unique name. Generally, file names should begin with an alphabetic character and be relatively short (e.g., six characters or less). Before a file can be used with a program, it should be *opened*. The act of opening a file prepares it for use. If the data in the file are to be read, the file should be opened for input. On the other hand, if a file is to be used for output, it should be erased prior to use. Erasure is accomplished by opening the file for output.

To open a file for input, you must usually have a statement in your program such as:

10   OPEN "PRICES", IN

This will prepare the file name "PRICES" for reading (input).

To open a file for output requires a statement such as:

20   OPEN "VALUES", OUT

This cleans out any previous contents of file "VALUES" and prepares the file to receive output. Once a file has been opened for output, it is a simple matter to store information in it. For example:

30   PUT "VALUES", Z

adds the number currently stored in variable Z to the file. And:

40   PUT "VALUES", A, C, F$

adds the values contained in variables A, C, and F$ to the file.

When all desired items have been stored in the output file, it should be *closed*. This is simple enough:

50   CLOSE "VALUES"

Items may be read from an input file in a manner similar to that used to read items from data statements. For example:

60   GET "PRICES", A, B9, X(3), A$

This will get the value of A from the input file "PRICES", then the value of B9, then X(3), and finally, A$. If later the program encounters the statement:

70   GET "PRICES", X5

the next item in the input file will be assigned to X5. It is not necessary that you use the same variable names that you used when the file was created; hence, you may have earlier used the name R3 instead of X5 for the item above. The only requirement is that you be sure that the data in the file and the variables to which they are assigned are of the same type. Never try to "GET" a string from a file, for example, and "PUT" it into a numeric variable.

When all desired items have been read from the input file, simply say:

80   CLOSE "PRICES"

It is not always necessary to use the "CLOSE" statement, since the computer usually closes your files after your program has been executed. However, you may wish to switch an input file to output (or vice versa) during the course of the program. If you do that, then you must use the "CLOSE" statement before you "OPEN" the file again.

In many systems, you may have several files—both input and output—open at one time. To reduce the number of "OPEN" and "CLOSE" statements you must write, you can usually open or close more than one file with a single statement, as in:

$$OPEN \text{ "WHO", "WHAT", "HOW", "WHY", IN}$$
$$CLOSE \text{ "NEVER", "AGAIN"}$$

The first of these statements opens four input files; the second closes two (input and/or output) files at once.

One other useful feature: The end-of-file clause—used with input files—can be very handy when you are not sure how many items you will find. Suppose you are processing a weekly payroll file and your program cannot assume that there will always be the same number of employees each week. In this case, it may happen that you will ask the computer to "GET" the next set of data and there won't be any more. The solution is to write:

$$GET \text{ "PAY", N\$, W, H, EOF 450}$$

This statement instructs the computer to read N\$, W, and H from the input file "PAY", and if it is unable to do so because there are no more data items, to branch to statement 450. The notation "EOF" is shorthand for "end of file."

To illustrate the usefulness of files, we will construct a small part of an *information retrieval* system. The information in question concerns grades. First, we will prepare a file named "GRADES", containing the following information:

Number of students in the class
Number of examinations given
Name of student
Score on first examination
   •
   •
Score on last examination   }   information for
                                             first student

Name of student
Score on first examination
   •
   •
Score on last examination   }   information for
                                             second student
   •
   •
   •

Name of student
Score on first examination
- •
- •
Score on last examination

} information for
last student

Here is a program to create the file and obtain the needed information from the terminal:

```
 5    REM -- PROGRAM TO PREPARE A FILE OF GRADES
10    OPEN "GRADES",OUT
20    PRINT "HOW MANY STUDENTS IN THE CLASS";
21    INPUT N
22    PUT "GRADES",N
30    PRINT "HOW MANY EXAMINATIONS HAVE BEEN GIVEN";
31    INPUT M
32    PUT "GRADES",M
40    PRINT "NOW GIVE ME THE STUDENT DATA";
41    PRINT
50    FOR I = 1 TO N
52      PRINT "STUDENT NAME";
54      INPUT N$
56      PUT "GRADES",N$
60      FOR J = 1 TO M
62        PRINT "SCORE ON EXAM";J;
64        INPUT S
66        PUT "GRADES",S
68      NEXT J
70    NEXT I
80    CLOSE "GRADES"
90    END
```

After this program has been run, the desired information will be tucked away safely in the file named "GRADES". Barring some sort of catastrophe, it will be there later on, whenever needed, for use with any program.

Knowing this, we can prepare a program to print the grades of any student:

```
  5    REM -- PROGRAM TO FIND A STUDENT'S GRADES
 10    OPEN "GRADES",IN
 20    PRINT "WHAT STUDENT ARE YOU INTERESTED IN";
 22    INPUT N$
 30    GET "GRADES",N,M
 40    FOR I = 1 TO N
 42      GET "GRADES",S$
 44      IF S$ = N$ THEN 100
 46      REM -- THIS IS NOT THE STUDENT, READ GRADES AND GO ON
 48      FOR J = 1 TO M
 50        GET "GRADES",S
 52      NEXT J
 60    NEXT I
 70    REM -- STUDENT NOT FOUND AT ALL
 72    PRINT "SORRY -- THIS STUDENT ISN'T IN THE CLASS"
 74    STOP
100    REM -- STUDENT FOUND, GET AND PRINT GRADES
```

```
110    PRINT "GRADES FOLLOW --"
120    FOR J = 1 TO M
122      GET "GRADES",S
124      PRINT "SCORE ON EXAM";J;" WAS ";S
126    NEXT J
128    CLOSE "GRADES"
130    END
```

Note that items in the file must be read one by one, even though some of them may be uninteresting (e.g., those read in line numbers 48 through 52).

Once a file of grades is available, all sorts of useful programs can be created to deal with it. For example:

A program to compute average scores for students and/or for the class as a whole.

A program to print the names of students currently failing the course (i.e., with average scores below some predetermined value).

A program to create a new file, using the data from the old file plus any changes entered by the user (e.g., those owing to errors in grading).

A program to create a new file, using the data from the old file plus the scores received on the latest examination given.

A program to determine overall scores at the end of the term, to prepare a list of students ranked from the highest to the lowest score, and (possibly) to assign letter grades.

If each program in the set were truly conversational, the result could (and undoubtedly would) be called a complete grading *system*. And it could be used by virtually anyone.

Clearly, the availability of file storage makes possible a whole range of new applications. Many are tremendously valuable. This is just as well, since file storage may be scarce and/or expensive. But it is often well worth the cost.

Problems

1. Using the IF . . . THEN . . . ELSE statement, write the shortest program segment possible to set variable S to: -1 if X is negative, 0 if X is zero, and $+1$ if X is positive.

2. A well-to-do programmer uses a computer to help him remember important dates. Every morning he types in the month, date, and day of the week. The computer then tells him what, if anything, is expected of him. Here is a partial list of the days that are crucial and the messages to be printed:

day	*message*
any Friday the 13th	BE CAREFUL
July 2	THIS IS YOUR ANNIVERSARY
July 14	IT'S BASTILLE DAY
any Sunday	GO SAILING

(a) Write a program to obtain the month, date, and day of the week from the user, then print any applicable messages. Assume that your system allows logical expressions with AND and OR.

(b) The programmer really has the relevant information stored in a file called "DATES", in the following format:

> month
> date
> day
> message
>
> month
> date
> day
> message
> •
> •
> •
> month
> date
> day
> message

Every entry is stored as a string of characters. If an item is not relevant, an asterisk is used. For example:

> " * "
> "13"
> "FRIDAY"
> "BE CAREFUL"
> " * "
> " * "
> "SUNDAY"
> "GO SAILING"

Rewrite your program so that it can use this file. Assume there could be any numbers of entries contained in the file.

3. Using the file "GRADES" described in this chapter, write a program to add the scores for a new examination to the file. You will first have to create a new file, then copy it back into the old file. Remember that after closing a file used for one purpose (i.e., input or output), you may reopen it again for another purpose.

Answers

1. Some systems allow you to use an IF statement after THEN or ELSE. If yours is one of them, you can get the job done in one line:

$$\text{IF } X < 0 \quad \text{THEN } S = -1 \text{ ELSE} \quad \text{IF } X = 0 \text{ THEN } S = 0 \text{ ELSE } S = 1$$

A more prosaic approach would use two statements:

$$\text{IF } X < 0 \quad \text{THEN } S = -1 \quad \text{ELSE } S = 0$$
$$\text{IF } X > 0 \quad \text{THEN } S = 1$$

2. (a) There is nothing very complicated about this, especially with AND. Here is a program to do the job:

```
10    PRINT "MONTH";
11    INPUT M$
20    PRINT "DATE";
21    INPUT T$
30    PRINT "DAY OF THE WEEK";
31    INPUT D$
40    REM -- CHECK FOR APPLICABLE MESSAGES
41    IF (D$="FRIDAY") AND (T$="13") THEN PRINT "BE CAREFUL"
42    IF (M$="JULY") AND (T$="2") THEN PRINT "THIS IS YOUR ANNIVERSARY"
43    IF (M$="JULY") AND (T$="14") THEN PRINT "IT'S BASTILLE DAY"
44    IF D$="SUNDAY" THEN PRINT "GO SAILING"
50    REM -- THAT'S ALL
60    END
```

Note that every possibility must be checked, since more than one message may apply (e.g., if Bastille Day falls on a Sunday).

(b) This is almost as straightforward:

```
5     REM -- GET INFORMATION FROM USER
10    PRINT "MONTH";
11    INPUT M$
20    PRINT "DATE";
21    INPUT T$
30    PRINT "DAY OF THE WEEK";
31    INPUT D$
40    REM -- OPEN FILE
41    OPEN "DATES", IN
50    REM -- GET MONTH, DATE, DAY, AND MESSAGE FROM FILE
61    GET "DATES", W$, X$, Y$, Z$, EOF 100
```

```
70    REM -- CHECK TO SEE IF MESSAGE IS APPLICABLE
71    REM -- IF IT IS NOT, GO BACK TO READ ANOTHER RECORD
72    IF (W$<>"*") AND (W$<>M$) THEN 50
74    IF (X$<>"*") AND (X$<>T$) THEN 50
76    IF (Y$<>"*") AND (Y$<>D$) THEN 50
80    REM -- THIS IS AN APPLICABLE MESSAGE, PRINT IT
81    PRINT Z$
82    GO TO 50
100   REM -- ALL ENTRIES HAVE BEEN CHECKED
110   PRINT "THAT'S ALL"
115   CLOSE "DATES"
120   END
```

Line 61 reads each set of entries. At the end of the file, the program must be brought to its conclusion since there is no more work to do.

Lines 72 through 76 check to see if the current message applies. It does not apply if any entry from the file that is not an asterisk does not match the corresponding item for the current day. This is not the only way to perform the required tests, but it is a way that does not require a statement exceeding the length of a normal line. Some systems allow statements to continue on a second line. If you have such a system, you can write something like this:

> IF   ((W$ = " * ") OR (W$ = M$))   AND ((X$ = " * ") OR
> (X$ = T$))   AND ((Y$ = " *") OR (Y$ = D$))
> THEN 80   ELSE   50

This single (but long) statement can replace the three statements in lines 72, 74, and 76.

3. Here's a program that tells the instructor each student's name, then stores away the new grade as soon as the instructor types it. Afterward, the new file is copied back into "GRADES", replacing the previous contents.

```
10    REM -- OPEN CURRENT FILE
11    OPEN "GRADES", IN
20    REM -- OPEN A TEMPORARY FILE FOR THE REVISED VERSION
21    OPEN "TEMP", OUT
30    REM -- GET THE NUMBER OF STUDENTS
31    GET "GRADES", N
32    REM -- PUT THE NUMBER OF STUDENTS ON THE NEW FILE
33    PUT "TEMP", N
40    REM -- GET THE CURRENT NUMBER OF EXAMS
41    GET "GRADES", M
42    REM -- PUT THE NEW NUMBER OF EXAMS ON THE NEW FILE
43    PUT "TEMP", M+1
50    REM -- GET THE OLD INFORMATION FOR EACH STUDENT
51    REM -- THEN PUT IT AND THE NEW INFORMATION ON THE NEW FILE
60    FOR I = 1 TO N
62      REM -- GET AND PUT THE STUDENT'S NAME
63      GET "GRADES", N$
64      PUT "TEMP", N$
```

```
70      REM -- GET AND PUT THE OLD GRADES
72      FOR J = 1 TO M
73        GET "GRADES", S
74        PUT "TEMP", S
75      NEXT J
80      REM -- GET AND PUT THE NEW GRADE
81      PRINT "GRADE FOR";N$;
82      INPUT G
83      PUT "TEMP", G
84    NEXT I
100   REM -- THE NEW FILE IS ALL SET, CLOSE BOTH FILES
110   CLOSE "GRADES", "TEMP"
200   REM -- NOW OPEN THEM FOR COPYING
210   OPEN "TEMP", IN
211   OPEN "GRADES", OUT
220   REM -- COPY INFORMATION FROM "TEMP" INTO "GRADES"
230   GET "TEMP", N, M
231   PUT "GRADES", N, M
240   FOR I = 1 TO N
242     GET "TEMP", N$
243     PUT "GRADES", N$
245     FOR J = 1 TO M
246       GET "TEMP", S
247       PUT "GRADES", S
248     NEXT J
250   NEXT I
300   REM -- ALL SET
310   CLOSE "GRADES", "TEMP"
320   END
```

Index

Index